Hoover Institution Studies: 30

Communism in Japan

A Case of Political Naturalization

COMPARATIVE COMMUNIST PARTY POLITICS

Jan F. Triska, Editor

Communism in Japan

A Case of Political Naturalization

Paul F. Langer

Hoover Institution Press
Stanford University
Stanford, California

The Hoover Institution on War, Revolution and Peace, founded at Stanford University in 1919 by the late President Herbert Hoover, is a center for advanced study and research on public and international affairs in the twentieth century. The views expressed in its publications are entirely those of the authors and do not necessarily reflect the views of the Hoover Institution.

Contents

Preface

This monograph on the postwar Japanese Communist Party is one of several in a series of comparative studies of non-ruling Communist parties undertaken under the auspices of the Institute of Political Studies of Stanford University. To permit maximum comparability, the author has followed as closely as possible the agreed-upon outline of the structure of all studies in the series. Inevitably, this has imposed constraints upon the organization of the material and occasionally has resulted in some repetition.

The student of Japanese Communist affairs—quite in contrast to the student of other non-ruling Communist parties in Asia—is confronted with a veritable *embarras de richesse* of research materials. This study does not claim to have exhausted them all, but it is based on a wide range of Japanese language documents, primarily materials issued by the Japanese Communist Party and the Japanese government. The selected bibliography notes only a few of these, since a full listing would be both very long and of interest only to the specialist.

To enhance readability, Japanese terms have been used only when it seemed essential. Otherwise the English equivalent has been preferred. Proper names follow Japanese order, i.e., family name first, then given name.

This study may show the traces of having been written over a period of more than a year and in a variety of locations from California to Elba, Italy. An effort has been made, however, to update the text and to give it consistency.

Paul F. Langer

July, 1971

Editor's Introduction

This study of the Japanese Communist Party is one of a series of monographs which together comprise comparative politics of non-ruling Communist parties (NRCPs). The series is concerned with the state of the non-ruling Communist parties in the world, with the causes of their emergence, and in particular with the question: *Why are NRCPs strong in some national states and not in others?* The theoretical focus of the series is on (a) the *varieties* of the NRCPs and their individual mutations and variations from the prescriptive Bolshevik organizational model; (b) the *causes* of these varieties, and identification of those environments within which NRCPs operate which have been most variety-productive; and (c) the *consequences* of these varieties, i.e., the particular conditions these varieties have produced which make for similarities or differences among the NRCPs.

The series examines three major assumptions:

1) Traditionally, whatever its immediate objectives and preoccupations, every NRCP has professed the principal long-range aspiration of becoming a ruling party, i.e., each has hoped to follow the path of those parties which—like the Czechoslovak, the Yugoslav, the Polish, or the Chinese party—became ruling Communist parties (RCPs). However, the less an NRCP is willing to sponsor solely the interests of the RCPs, the more it tends to deviate from this aspiration. Moreover, the peaceful coexistence strategy of the U.S.S.R. since the Twentieth Congress of the CPSU has not supported the aspiration of the NRCPs to all-out struggle for power in their national states.

2) The NRCPs tend to be progressively more nationally than internationally oriented, and their national orientation tends to increase in direct proportion to the growing disunity among the RCPs (a result, in turn, of the proliferation of RCPs in the world). The NRCPs, in other words, are—like the RCPs—subject to growing positive interaction with their immediate operational environment and hence become progressively less heterogeneous with their national environment. (If an NRCP is small, weak, and operating in an indifferent or hostile national environment, it is probable that its cadres are almost completely alienated from its national environment, and that its perceived operational environment is an extension of that perceived by the ruling Communist parties.)

3) The greater the coincidence between means and/or goals of an NRCP and its operational environment, the more influential the NRCP. NRCPs have declined or been unsuccessful in those countries—such as Ireland, Canada, and the United States—where their operational environment has been unalterably hostile; they have gained or been successful in those parts of the world where they have adjusted to their operational environment—as in Italy and France—or where the operational environment has favored NRCP means and/or goals, as in Asia. (NRCPs operating in an unfriendly environment in developing nations and which side with the Chinese Communist Party in advocating uprisings and violence in underdeveloped countries create a danger of general war which the peaceful coexistence policy of the U.S.S.R. was designed to avoid.)

Among other assumptions examined empirically in the series—some of them current in the various writings on the subject—are the following: "Communism breeds on poverty and underdevelopment"; "The achievements of communism are the achievements of organization"; "Communist ideology is an imperfect theory of modernization"; and "The behavior of an NRCP is determined by its functions within its operational environment."

In the sense that "freedom of formation of associations to seek to control the state prevails only in the Western democracies and in states modeled after them,"[1] the NRCPs are *political parties* in those states where such freedom, however minimal, exists; but even in nondemocratic states they have competitors for rule. The NRCPs differ from the RCPs not only in that the ruling parties are not parties at all in the above sense, but they are by definition without competitors for rule. This difference has important consequences: the extant political and social system usually has a far greater impact on an NRCP than on an RCP, while the relative impact of the NRCP on its operational (national) environment is normally incomparably smaller. This difference is observable and measurable in the social composition of the NRCPs; in their structures, operational codes, and strategies; and in their relations with other CPs, both ruling and non-ruling.

What constitutes a Communist party? Some Communist parties call themselves communist, whereas others, such as the Irish Workers' League, are truly communist in all save name. Still others, such as the Mexican Workers' and Farmers' Party, have strong communist leanings but exist independently of, and sometimes in competition with, the local Communist party. Some countries have both a Communist party-states oriented party and a "national" Communist party; some countries have these plus a Trotskyite party. Where communism is illegal, numerous left-wing parties may preach Marxist slogans but maintain few connections with the Communist party-states.

We are concerned here only with those parties which perceive themselves to be a part of the world Communist movement and are so perceived by the party-states, thus automatically excluding all Trotskyite and "national" Communist parties, as well as left-wing parties which do not acknowledge the party-states' leadership. Furthermore, we count only one party per country, selecting that party most closely identified with the Communist system.

The common outline divides each study into six principal parts: The first two comprising Chapter I of this volume concern the historical setting, concentrating on the emergence, evolution, and organizational strength of the NRCP. Here we search for causal relations—why and how an NRCP came into being, which phenomena influenced its evolution; which developments contributed to its strength. The third section (Chapter II) deals with the NRCP in terms of its role and organization, i.e., its status, membership, and structure. Chapter III has to do with the NRCP national environment (its geographic and demographic locale, and the prevailing social, political, economic, military, belief, and other relevant systems). The intercourse between the NRCP and its national environment, and hence the past and present national operational code of the NRCP, are treated in Chapter IV. Chapter V deals with the NRCP's international operational code. And Chapter VI stipulates the principal determinants of the NRCP's behavior. In addition, the Introduction to the case study concentrates on what the author believes to be the unique features of his particular NRCP, what distinguishes it from other national parties. The Summary and Conclusions (Chapter VII) briefly review the high spots of the case study, emphasizing causal explanations of the NRCP's emergence, its strength, and its present orientation.

A few additional words concerning some of the components of the outline are in order.

First, there has been no attempt made as yet to span the gaps between models constructed by three authors who have made important theoretical contributions to the study of NRCPs, namely Gabriel Almond,[2] Hadley Cantrill,[3] and Lucian Pye.[4] Chapter II should remedy this deficiency, at least in part, by emphasizing *role* and *status* of the party. That chapter describes functions of the NRCP which are assumed to signify the (roughly) three stages of party development:

1) In developing nations—in non-politicized, non-community societies—revolutionary NRCPs are a dynamic force. Here they perform, in addition to their own unique objectives, the role of socializers toward modernity.[5] Here they feed the aspirations and ambitions of persons frustrated by an economy that cannot accommodate their skills. The high want/get ratio resulting from such economic conditions, we hypothesize, both alienates and brings into the CP those wishing to transform their societies rapidly and make them part of the modern world.

2) In societies where only some segments of the population have not been integrated and incorporated into the social and political system, the NRCPs attempt to integrate alienated (political and social) individuals for articulation of their dissatisfaction and protest. These *sub-cultural* NRCPs, habituated to defending the negative interests of isolated sections of the society, function more as *social* parties than as political parties. Seton-Watson has described what happened when a sub-cultural NRCP left the protest field to enter responsible government in post-war France: The Communists had traditionally viewed the parliament as a useful forum for propaganda, and "it was not easy to discard this mentality. Denunciation and demagogy were easier and more enjoyable than responsibility."[6]

3) Finally, when NRCPs have gone beyond social protest and assumed political responsibility, their deviant and revolutionary character tends to be replaced by legitimacy and social plausibility, and their difference from other political parties tends to be reduced, sometimes to zero. From an ideological protest movement, the *electoral* NRCP tends to become a pragmatic and non-heretic political force. Italian and French CPs are probably the outstanding examples of NRCPs in this stage of operation.

The third part of the study (Chapter II) also focuses on status: Is the NRCP *influential*? (What is its political weight?) Is it *militant*? (Has a militant politics normally farther-reaching consequences within the immediate political process?) Is it *tolerated*? (Might the same NRCP be perceived as radical in one system and conservative in another?) Is it *changing* its status? (What are the NRCP elite's present aspirations as compared to those of yesterday? How flexible is the elite's perception of its own role? Could an NRCP typology rank-order NRCPs according to their willingness to experiment and change their organizational forms?) And what are its *prospects*? (Does the NRCP "have a future"?) Inasmuch as all these variables have negative counterparts, twenty different combinations are possible, from one extreme (influential, militant, tolerated, changing NRCPs with positive prospects) to the other (non-influential [impotent], bargain-oriented, not tolerated, unchanging NRCPs with negative prospects).

With appropriate indicators, the several NRCP types may be of research value in further refining the NRCP types in the world and then matching the differences with (a) the kind of membership-leadership, rank and file, and supporters they attract; (b) socialization processes within the NRCPs; (c) environmental conditions as correlated with party transition from one type to another; etc.

As to the structure of the NRCP: Scholars (e.g., Duverger[7]) often assume that CPs are rigid hierarchial orders, that the party occupies the whole time of its elites, and that the party organization does not allow its members to participate fully in ordinary ways in the wider social community. Party demands create a rigid personality type, and the party recruits personalities predisposed to fit easily into the party order.

But is this true of the new parties whose leaders were recruited at the end of the Stalin era and have no personal experience of the Comintern organization in its last years? The major figures in the Cuban party, for instance, all began their party careers in the last years of the Stalin era or later, as did many, perhaps most, of the leaders of sub-Saharan parties, the Burmese party, and many of the newer Latin American parties. Is it not possible that these new leaders will diverge from the old stereotype? If they are not rigid authoritarian personalities and if their party organizations are more flexible, leaders now may be more readily responsive to environmental influences than were those of the Stalinist period. New parties with youthful leadership also should be more eclectic in their regard for the history of the CPSU, the Comintern, etc., and more willing to experiment with new strategies and new relationships with other political groups. The Sino-Soviet split should foster such eclecticism.

Chapter III describes attributes in the environment that may make the objective of the NRPC, namely its transformation into an RCP, possible or easy. For instance, is the political system similar in some respects to that in a Communist party-state: dictatorial, one-party, controlled press, etc.? Is the economy largely government controlled? Does the environment present problems similar to those solved more or less successfully by the CP in China, in the Soviet Union, or in Yugoslavia? Are the relations between the state and the Soviet Union and/or China and/or Yugoslavia friendly and conducive to the growth of a local CP organization, or favorable to the growth of non-communist parties and groups that partially imitate Soviet or Chinese organizations and methods?

The social fabric, and in particular the social structure, of a given country is an important factor affecting the success of an NRCP. If there is little divergence in primordial loyalties within a country, the effectiveness of Communist appeal to primordial sentiments is likely to be slight. The more recent difficulties of CPs in the Middle East, for example, might be due in part to shifts in Communist appeals from intellectuals to class loyalties in nations relatively lacking in ethnic diversity.

As to the political system, both Max Weber[8] and Duverger have stressed the "natural emergence" of parties, given certain conditions in the political environment of a given state. Weber's formulation of party evolution encompasses as causative factors both the development of a national legislature and the growth in size of the electorate. Duverger, whose work is perhaps more relevant for the study of NRCPs, deals in part with externally created parties which emerge outside the legislature and invariably pose some sort of challenge to the ruling group, particularly in terms of representation. Duverger also stresses that externally created parties may be associated with (1) expanded suffrage, (2) strongly articulated secular or religious ideologies, or (3) nationalistic or anti-colonial movements. This broader handling of causality is more applicable to a study of NRCPs because their development may well deviate from any general pattern in response to partisan strategies devised by one or more Communist party-states.

The concern with party organization is widespread in the literature. Sigmund Neuman,[9] for example, postulates that one of the functions of the modern society is to transform parties of individual representation into parties of integration. Duverger's overly complex scheme of party organizations may be contrasted with overly simplified concepts, such as the dichotomous schemes of Thomas Hodgkin ("elite parties" vs. "parties of personalities")[10]; Ruth Schachter ("patron parties" vs.

"mass parties")[11] ; Martin Kilson ("caucus-type parties" vs. "mass-type parties")[12] ; or even John Kautsky ("traditionalist nationalists" vs. "modernist nationalists")[13.] However, such typologies, while useful in ranking parties along a single continuum, are not necessarily useful for our purpose of explaining the relations between environmental influences and the changing organizational structures and behavior patterns of NRCPs. Here the linkage between NRCP characteristics and environmental influences are especially important.

A number of creative people have contributed to this series. In addition to the authors of the series, in this case Professor Paul F. Langer, I would like to thank Wallace Berry, Jack Kangas, Carole Norton, Noralou Roos, John Rue, and Maurice Simon for their imaginative contributions and valuable assistance.

Jan F. Triska

Stanford University
July, 1971

Introduction

After studying the record of the Japanese Communist Party (JCP), the student of international communism may conclude that there is little in it that could be termed unique. Yet there are certain distinctive features of the JCP, results of the uniqueness of the Party's national environment, that set it apart both from the advanced countries of the West and from the less modernized countries of Asia.

Alone among major Asian nations, Japan escaped colonial domination by the West. Only Japan among the countries of Asia successfully embarked on a race with the Western nations for colonial domain. In contrast to Communist movements in other parts of Asia, therefore, the Japanese Communists could never play on an anti-colonial, anti-imperialist theme—except against their own government. They were thus unable to ride the crest of anti-Western nationalism as did other revolutionary movements in Asia. In its inability to utilize nationalism—at least until quite recently—the JCP therefore resembles the Communist parties of the West rather than those of Asia.

The Japanese Communists also had to operate under conditions quite unlike those in other Asian countries, for Japan alone in Asia was capable of modernizing rapidly and successfully enough to attain the technological level of the West. Thus, the Japanese Communists faced some conditions we consider typical of the advanced nations of the West, but other conditions that bound them to Asia by geography and cultural-emotional heritage. This may explain why increasingly the Japanese Communists appear to be combining two contradictory strategies, one of militancy and ideological purity which we associate with the revolutionary movements of continental Asia, and the other a pragmatic search for an adjustment to the national environment of a developed and prosperous country.

The Japanese Party has differed the most from its Western counterparts, at least until very recently, in the extent and duration of its alienation from its national environment. This alienation was forced upon the Party in prewar times by the repressive nature of the Japanese state it faced and by the causally related and long-lasting Soviet control over its leadership and policies. Only in the last few years has the JCP freed itself from these and other restrictive foreign bonds to act as an autonomous party in domestic as well as in international affairs. One might say that the Japanese Communist Party, when compared with the Communist parties of the West, is a case of retarded development due primarily to unfavorable historical conditions.

Comparing the JCP with the domestic political forces with which it must compete, the Party distinguishes itself by a firm and dogmatic belief in the universal validity of the ideological foundations on which it rests and its perception of having a dual role. First, it is an actor on the Japanese scene which it seeks to reshape in line with Marxist-Leninist convictions, but also, in contrast to other Japanese parties (which may actually share some of its beliefs, as do the Japanese Socialists), it acts as part of an evolving Communist world system which imposes on the Party duties and responsibilities transcending its national framework.

1: The Prewar Past

Marxist thought in Japan dates back to the last decade of the nineteenth century, when it was introduced from the West as one of several socialist theories that aroused the interest of Japanese intellectuals who were critical of their country's social and political order. Marxism came to be one of the many diverse components, none of them neatly delineated or organized, of the incipient Japanese socialist movement. Within this movement, Marxism contended for preeminence with two more influential trends, a moderate Christian and humanist type of socialism on the one hand and radical, revolutionary anarcho-syndicalism on the other. The imperial government police virtually eradicated the latter groups on the eve of World War I, although anarcho-syndicalist ideas continued for another decade to compete with Marxist thought among Japanese intellectuals and revolutionaries, particularly among labor. Christian socialism, however, marked socialist thinking in Japan for several decades, although its influence has gradually waned; it is to this day an important part of the heritage of the moderate wings of Japan's two socialist parties, the Japan Socialist Party (JSP) and the Democratic Socialist Party (DSP).

Marxism really came into its own in Japan during and immediately after World War I. This was the time when Japan's rapid transformation into an industrial society and the parallel growth of a labor movement, the increasingly glaring inequities of the nation's social and political system, and severe economic fluctuations combined with the influx of radical literature and ideas from abroad—primarily from the United States and Western Europe—to impel many reformist socialists toward acceptance of the class struggle and other Marxist revolutionary tenets. This developing trend was powerfully stimulated by the Bolshevik Revolution, which marked a turning point in the history of socialist thought in Japan. From that time, it is possible to speak of a Communist movement in Japan, even though it took several more years to be organized.

To many Japanese intellectuals, the case of Russia, and of Lenin's revolution there, seemed directly relevant to Japan. They compared their own Emperor system to the rule of the Tsars and equated Japan's rigid class structure with seemingly similar conditions in Russia. They detected other parallels in the problems faced by the Russian and Japanese peoples, including those posed by absentee landownership, the transition from semi-feudal agrarian to industrial societies, sharp distinctions between the privileged and underprivileged, and particularly the oppressive weight of the military and police apparatus on the people's freedom of expression.

An organized Marxist Communist movement made its appearance in Japan on July 15, 1922. It took the form of an illegal, secret Communist Party functioning as a branch of the Comintern, and the date of its appearance is considered the official birthday of the Japanese Communist Party (JCP). The Party owed its establishment to foreign—particularly Comintern—influence and guidance. (It must be recalled that to the Russian Bolsheviks Japan was a key country, since Japanese armed forces occupied much of eastern Russia and seemed in a position to threaten the survival of the Bolshevik regime.)

The actual founding of the JCP was the result of joint efforts by several Japanese Marxists who had been living abroad (mostly in the United States), where they had contact with foreign Communists, and by a few resident Japanese radicals. Representatives of both groups were invited to participate in an international Communist meeting in Soviet Russia in preparation for the establishment of a Japanese branch of the Comintern. Typical of the first group was the well-known former Christian Socialist Katayama Sen, who had resided in the United States since 1914 after serving a term in a Japanese prison for anti-government activities. In the United States Katayama became acquainted with American Communists and Russian political exiles, including Trotsky and Bukharin. By then a confirmed Leninist, he joined the U.S. Communist party in 1919 and became the central figure in a small Japanese Communist group of exiles. Two years later, responding to a Comintern invitation, Katayama went to Soviet Russia, where he played a major role at the First Congress of the Toilers of the East (1922). Thereafter, as Asia's best-known Communist among those active in international propaganda and as a faithful follower of Comintern directives, he spent the rest of his life (he died in the 1930's) at Comintern headquarters in Moscow, advising on Communist strategy and propaganda in Asia.

Katayama was joined by a number of Japanese radicals who were selected by a Comintern emissary to go to Moscow.[1] Among this group was Tokuda Kyūichi, who was to play a prominent role in the Japanese Communist movement for the rest of his life (at the time of his death in Communist China in the 1950's, Tokuda was Secretary General of the Party). Tokuda and a small group of Japanese delegates returned to Japan in 1922 after having received funds, instructions, and theoretical guidance from Comintern officials. Their mission was to set up a Japanese branch of the Comintern. The new party was soon joined by Nosaka Sanzō, typical in his thorough exposure to foreign Communist influence of the men who were to lead the Communist organization in Japan. Of middle-class origin (as were many of his associates), well educated, and once a Socialist reformer rather than a revolutionary, Nosaka had become a charter member of the British Communist Party while he was in England in 1920 and then attended the Far Eastern People's Congress in Russia before returning to Japan in 1922. He was subsequently important as a link between the JCP and the international Communist movement centered in Moscow, serving first as Katayama's deputy at Comintern headquarters and eventually as his successor there until he moved to China during World War II. He spent several years with the Chinese Communists, returning to Japan in 1946. Nosaka is now the Chairman of the Japanese Communist Party.

There is ample evidence for the conclusion that the JCP emerged as an organization in direct response to and with the assistance of the Comintern. The Party was not, however, a wholly artificial foreign creation; it was the natural culmination of an intellectual evolution to Marxist-Leninist revolutionary thought out of distress over the inequities in the Japanese political and social system and frustration over attempts at peaceful reform.

EVOLUTION OF THE PARTY

The JCP operated as an illegal and secret organization from 1922 until the mid-1930's, when the Japanese government's repression finally either made most Communists recant or forced them into exile or prison. During its brief prewar life,[2] the Party was so weakened by mass arrests and internal factionalism that it could operate only intermittently and was unable to provide continuity of leadership, organization, and strategy. Throughout these difficult years, the organization depended heavily on outside—primarily Soviet—support for its survival. In contrast to the vast majority of the Japanese people, the Japanese Communists generally did not view such assistance or the policy guidance they received from abroad as objectionable. In prewar Japan, the JCP operated as the branch of the Comintern that it had been founded to be.*

Any tendency to evolve in the direction of a truly national political party was stifled by the mutually reinforcing constraints of the national and international environments in which the Communists were forced to operate. While the degree of severity with which the Japanese government and Japanese society in general rejected the Communist program and repressed Communist and pro-Communist activity varied during the Party's prewar life, the Japanese Communists were never permitted to emerge from underground and develop into a legal political party. Circumstances condemned them to a furtive existence on the fringes of Japanese society. This state of isolation from Japanese reality was further aggravated by the continuing and pervasive Soviet influence over the JCP.

In the years between the world wars, Party strategy (as evidenced in the major 1927 and 1932 theses) was formulated in Moscow by Soviet and other foreign Communist leaders. Thus, it reflected faithfully the shifts in Soviet strategy and the changes in Soviet leadership and outlook rather than changing conditions in Japan itself. Japanese Party leaders were removed or appointed at the behest of the Comintern, and their successors were trained in Moscow and then sent back into Japan with Comintern instructions. Under the circumstances, the Party could not evolve in such a way as to open channels of communication with the non-Communist left, for Stalinist guidance kept the Japanese Communists oriented toward the problems of Moscow rather than those of Tokyo and set as the JCP's principal objective the defense of Soviet national interests.

The Party's illegal status further widened the gap separating it from Japanese reality. The Japanese Communists' dedication to the

---

*This is not to say that the Party's relationship with the Comintern did not pose a problem for the Japanese Communists. In the late 1920's and early 1930's, some of them questioned this relationship and because of it left the Party. Further, an important segment of left-wing Japanese Socialism—the so-called *Rōnō-ha* or Labor-Farmer Faction—owes its existence largely to differences with the Comintern over strategy and tactics in Japan. Even Nosaka, reportedly, felt rather relieved when the Comintern was finally dissolved in 1943.

protection of foreign interests increased their alienation from the national environment, which became more and more dominated by an extreme form of nationalism. Therefore, many Japanese viewed the Communists as traitors to the Japanese people. It was the tragedy of the Japanese Communist Party that national and international influences combined to turn it increasingly into a small, narrow, closed organization. The Party's energies were absorbed in the struggle for survival, and its ability to participate meaningfully in Japan's political life was severely limited by dogmatic insistence on a revolutionary strategy and by a consistently pro-Soviet orientation, which in turn incurred the full force of government repression. To make matters worse, the Party's foreign sponsors' insistence on complete control over all aspects of JCP policies and activities stifled whatever initiative its leaders might otherwise have displayed.

Some indication of the unfulfilled potential of the prewar Party can be gained by noting its comparative success during short periods of relative liberalization (mostly during the 1920's), which sometimes coincided with an easing of direct Soviet intervention into the JCP's affairs. From about 40 men in 1922, the Party was able during such periods to build an organization of some 1,000 (secret) members. Communists then played an important role in the legal left-wing Labor-Farmer Party and actually elected one of their men (a secret Party member) to the Diet; they had a foothold among left-wing labor unions; and they exerted considerable influence among intellectuals and students. These promising beginnings, however, were not allowed to come to fruition because Japan veered increasingly toward a repressive police regime and Stalinist intervention in the JCP's affairs showed little understanding of Japanese conditions.

As police repression and Stalinist influence over the JCP grew in intensity during the 1930's, the Party turned again into a narrow, conspiratorial organization beset by internal factional squabbles of extreme violence and destructiveness. In the process it lost the support of all those who were of a liberal turn of mind and who were unwilling to live under rigid Party discipline or submit to dictates from abroad. Thereafter, only a hard core of extremists remained—ultra-radical intellectuals and activist revolutionaries—willing to pay any price to be considered "correct" and faithful Marxist-Leninists by their foreign friends.

The prewar Japanese Communists are thus a prime example of a Communist movement that is compelled to operate under inhospitable conditions and alienates itself further from potential sources of domestic support by acting as an instrument of a foreign power, thus placing itself in direct opposition to the forces of nationalism at home.

Only a few Japanese Communists survived the decade of ultranationalism and repression (1935-45), either in prison, hidden underground, or in exile. When they re-emerged to reconstitute the Party after World War II, they were tough but self-righteous men, dependent on foreign guidance; they viewed nationalism as an inimical force; they tended to overemphasize the need for absolute subordination to Party discipline and were obsessed with doctrinaire theoretical Marxist interpretations and notions of ideological purity. After more than a decade of divorce from Japanese reality, they were poorly equipped to adjust rapidly to an entirely new set of conditions. Unlike Communists in Europe, the Japanese Communists were scarcely exposed to the experience of a broad united front of left-wing forces.

Since 1945, the Party has been able to operate legally and without fear of repression; it can reach out toward the Japanese people in a climate of opinion that provides vastly more favorable conditions than in prewar times; and it is now able to act—if it so wishes—independently of foreign assistance and advice. As will be shown, the prewar Party leaders who remain in control of the organizational apparatus have sought to adapt to these new conditions and to learn from the experience of the past, but they have been severely hampered in this by their deeply ingrained prewar attitudes.

PREWAR PARTY ORGANIZATION AND LEADERSHIP

The prewar Party's organizational structure was weak because the government never allowed the Communists to operate legally and police persecution and control prevented them from developing even an effective underground apparatus. Operating in conspiratorial fashion, the Japanese Communists were unable to penetrate the agencies of the government. They had to be content with sporadic attempts to build up a Party organization from the few (never more than 1,000 and much of the time probably not exceeding 100) Party members—intellectuals and former workers—who were willing to risk continuing the unequal struggle against the extremely efficient and ruthless state apparatus.

Under these conditions, contacts with Communists abroad—primarily in the Soviet Union, but also in China, Korea, and the United

States—were difficult to maintain even during the relatively liberal and permissive 1920's, and became impossible as the Japanese police tightened control during the 1930's. By the middle of the decade the JCP was completely cut off from its foreign sponsors. In turn, this isolation prevented the regular flow of funds from abroad necessary to maintain Communist operations. Even internal Party communications beyond the limits of a single city, such as Tokyo or Osaka, were difficult because of police supervision. That the Party was nevertheless able, during the 1920's and early 1930's, to issue and distribute intermittently its Party organ, *Akahata* (Red Flag), must be considered a relative success.

Factionalism, which is a characteristic of Japanese political organizations in general, was rampant under these conditions and wrecked whatever Party organization had been developing between police raids. Within the small Party organization there was antagonism between the radical intellectuals and those who claimed a working-class background, and between members who had their base in eastern Japan and those who had organized in the western part of the country. In addition, the Party was split by bitter feuds over problems of Communist doctrine and the "correct" interpretation of the shifts in Soviet strategy and their implications for Japan.

Most of the time the JCP, in imitation of foreign Communist parties, maintained a Central Committee, regional Party bodies, and local cells. But in practice except for very short periods—months, not years—such an elaborate apparatus existed only on paper. What did exist was a group of leaders, a few cadres in the factories of the larger urban centers, and a very few followers in factories and among intellectuals—students, professors, writers—as well as a handful of members of peasant origin. Except for a brief period in the 1920's, the prewar Communist organization in Japan was thus composed of a large top and a very small popular base.

As for prewar Party leadership, the Party at no time produced a single charismatic leader who could have given it a sense of direction and cohesion. Perhaps the main reason for the absence of a Japanese Mao Tse-tung, a Ho Chi Minh, or even a D. N. Aidit (Indonesia) is that the major police raids of 1923, 1928, 1929, 1930, and 1932 (not to mention other minor ones) effectively removed whatever leadership was developing in the Party apparatus and never allowed any member sufficient time to build a power base.

But this explanation, convincing at first glance, may not tell the whole story; for it is striking that even under vastly more favorable postwar conditions, the Japanese Communist Party has failed to produce a leader of real stature. It could well be that the composition of the JCP's leadership has played an important role in this phenomenon. Those who led the Party in prewar times (and on the whole still direct it today) were largely radical intellectuals or quasi-intellectuals. They were more interested in being "right" in terms of Marxist-Leninist orthodoxy than in having power as such. These writers, scholars, artists, and students (many of the latter trained in the Soviet Union) lived in a world of ideas and abstractions, divorced from reality. The few who did not fit this pattern were essentially technicians of illegal activity and lacked the breadth and experience in larger matters to gain uncontested leadership of the Party.

Another reason for this absence of outstanding men in the Japanese Communist organization no doubt was that independent-minded men were soon removed from leading positions if they did not unhesitatingly follow the dictates of their Soviet mentors. As mentioned earlier, Party policy and strategy were made in Moscow, not in Tokyo, and recalcitrant Party leaders were dismissed by direct fiat from the Soviet authorities, who appointed new and more pliable men in their stead. A good example is the case of a gifted rebel, the intellectual Fukumoto Kazuo, who gained substantial influence within the Japanese Party during the mid-1920's and had the impertinence to criticize even Marx and Lenin and, by implication, some of the major figures in the Soviet movement. Called to Moscow to defend himself and his theories, he was overruled by Bukharin, who wrote a new thesis for the JCP (the 1927 Thesis) and removed Fukumoto from his position of influence on the Central Committee. (It is true that even in Japan opposition to "Fuku-motoism" had arisen among Communists by 1926, and that it was sympathetically transmitted to the Comintern by Jacob Janson, the Comintern representative in Japan.)

There was simply no place for independent thinking and action in the Comintern-directed JCP. Those who disagreed tended to leave the Party ranks, many of them to join one or another of the radical Socialist factions. Those who remained were men with strong loyalty toward Moscow, such as the late Secretary General Tokuda Kyūichi and, at least until fairly recently, his successor in that position, Miyamoto Kenji. Both men visited Moscow for instructions during the prewar period and readily accepted Comintern advice. Others, such as Nosaka Sanzō, the current Party Chairman, went abroad to serve international communism more directly while influencing Party strategy from their vantage point in Moscow. Still others, such as Hakamada Satomi—one of the two or three top figures in the Party in 1970—were trained in Moscow at the KUTV (Communist University of the Toilers of the East), the predecessor of Moscow's Lumumba University. All of them shared a foreign orientation and a lack of familiarity with real conditions in Japan.

To a lesser extent, these characteristics marked the Party's rank and file, although we know much less about them since no systematic study of their origins has been made. To judge by official Japanese police records, the ordinary Party member shared with his leaders a strong intellectual orientation: many were university students, writers, artists, and scholars during the 1920's. In the 1930's, the workers, of whom there had always been a few in the Communist ranks, probably increased somewhat in number, as many of the intellectuals either recanted because of police pressure or threw in their lot with ultranationalism.

The little we know about prewar Communist organization and activity in rural Japan suggests that only a small percentage of Party members had rural origins or actively promoted the Party among Japan's millions of underprivileged tenant farmers. Throughout the prewar years, however, the Party found some support among the two major minority groups of Japan: the "outcasts," victims of social and, in prewar times, also legal discrimination, and the Korean residents whom the Japanese authorities automatically classified as potentially subversive and placed under extremely tight and discriminatory police supervision.

During the 1920's, when police action and government policy still made it possible for left-wing—though non-Communist—proletarian organizations to function intermittently, the Japanese Communist Party made inroads in labor and organized politics. Between 1925 and about 1928 (the year of a major anti-Communist police campaign), the Labor Union Council of Japan, a smaller federation with 15,000 members, was under strong and at times controlling Party influence in leadership and policy. (It should be noted that in this and similar cases, the leadership was mostly drawn from quasi-intellectuals rather than from actual workers.) After the Council was dissolved by the government, an illegal successor organization operated for a while with diminished membership, yet under Communist influence.

During this same period of legalized proletarian activity, a proletarian party, the Labor-Farmer Party, with overlapping membership, also served as an auxiliary of the Japanese Communists. Its dissolution in 1928 and the general tightening of police controls over all pro- and quasi-Communist organizations thereafter deprived the Party of a political front.* Communist sympathizers were now almost exclusively confined to the cultural organizations (particularly those in the fields of literature and the arts) which have always provided major reservoirs in Japan for Communist proselytizing and support. Such organizations too eventually came under suspicion of being "un-Japanese," as they were generally sympathetic to Marxist theories and opposed Japan's invasion of the Asian continent in the 1930's. In the late 1930's these organizations disappeared as had the Communist Party apparatus before them. This left only scattered individuals with Communist sympathies, and even most of them were rounded up by the police and sent to prison. They could be released only if they recanted or "reformed" into fervent nationalists. The few who survived the rigors of prison were freed only after Japan's defeat, re-entering postwar intellectual life either as Socialists or as Communists.

Throughout the prewar period of illegal Party activity, the Japanese Communists faithfully adhered at least in theory to the Communist organizational principle of democratic centralism. As implemented in Japan, the emphasis was clearly on centralism rather than on democratic procedure, for neither the Soviet model nor the generally autocratic outlook of Japanese society favored democratic practices within the Party organization. However, two factors served to limit the tendency toward autocratic rule. In the first place, the difficulty of communication within the Communist underground apparatus, which constantly was in danger of being detected and destroyed by the police, provided Party members and lower cadres with opportunities for independent action. Secondly, the prewar Japanese Party reflected a traditional characteristic of Japanese feudal organization, i.e., the leader/supporter or boss/henchman relationship, although in the case of the JCP this was not normally based on regional, geographic affinity (as

---

*Orders from Moscow subsequently advised the Japanese Communists that the Labor-Farmer Party should not be re-established and that they should instead develop the JCP into a mass party.

it was in other Japanese political associations). Thus, within the prewar Party, there were a number of smaller component groups, each consisting of a leader surrounded by a circle of followers whose loyalty centered on the leader of the group rather than on the central Party leadership.

In view of the highly effective prewar Japanese police apparatus and the ruthless way in which it operated, it must be considered a success and an indication of the strength and conviction of the Japanese Communists that they were able to maintain any sort of organization during much of the 1920's and the early 1930's. The obstacles the Communists faced became increasingly harder to surmount. Eventually mere suspicion of Communist sympathies meant prison, and participation in Communist activity could, at least in legal theory, spell a death sentence. Communist organizational efforts were rendered difficult and finally impossible as potential sympathizers and the reservoir of support were eliminated: during the 1930's, the Japanese authorities rounded up not only Communists but eventually all Socialists and most of the liberal elements critical of one or another aspect of Japanese policy and of Japan's political and social system. Thus, from about 1935 to a decade later, when Japan had been defeated and its government liberalized, Japanese Communist organizational activity ceased altogether.

The prewar Communist effort in Japan might be termed a failure if measured in purely numerical terms or with regard to concrete political achievements, but it did lay a base on which the postwar Party was able to build and develop a substantial Party organization. The men who emerged from prison after a decade or more—men such as Miyamoto, Tokuda, Hakamada, and Shiga Yoshio—though marked by the illegal struggle and by long confinement had been toughened by that experience. They were unlikely ever to turn away from communism and could thus provide the revived Party almost immediately with an experienced and dedicated leadership.

The major self-inflicted failure of the prewar Japanese Communist Party was its inability, because of its foreign orientation and direction, to come to terms with the forces of Japanese nationalism. As the tide of nationalism rose during the 1930's, the Communists were forced into a role that made them appear to be the tools of a foreign power, the Soviet Union, to the majority of the Japanese people and even to those who had once been sympathetic to the Party's social goals. Thus, the Japanese Communist Party not only lost independent-minded leaders and supporters like Fukumoto; it also lost by desertion in the early and mid-1930's some of its most able leaders, among them Nabeyama Sadachika and Sano Manabu, men who could not reconcile their patriotic sentiments with the Party's absolute loyalty to the Soviet Stalinist regime.

Prewar Japanese Communist organizational activity was essentially a function of two major factors: the varying degree of police repression of Communist activity and Moscow's intervention in JCP affairs. Two major organizational periods are distinguished: the era when domestic conditions in Japan were relatively favorable to liberal movements and to their exploitation by the radical left including the Communists, and the period of the 1930's when growing militarist and ultranationalist tendencies tended to isolate and weaken all but those organizations that supported the militaristic, expansionist government. The first period coincided, at least in its first years, with the pre-Stalinist era. Although the prewar JCP was under direct Soviet influence as long as communication between Moscow and the Japanese Communists was possible, the hand of the Soviet leaders rested less heavily on the Party before Stalinism became the governing principle of Soviet policy. In the first period, the Party and its leaders were accountable to Moscow for their policies and actions but were still allowed some voice in their own affairs. During the latter period, direct Soviet injection of personnel and strategic advice increased steadily until the channels of communication were cut by the Japanese authorities and what remained of Japanese communism was left to its own devices.

Some of the more conspicuous documented examples of outside Communist interference in Japanese Communist organizational affairs deserve mention. In the mid-1920's, when the Party had dissolved itself to await a more propitious time for direct political action, it was instructed by the Comintern to reverse this decision and return to life. Later, the Comintern proceeded to appoint a new Japanese Central Committee after the above-mentioned rejection of the policy positions of the Party rebel Fukumoto. Thereafter, and as the older Party leadership disappeared in prison, the new leaders not only were selected by Moscow from afar but were sent into Japan after having been trained and tested in the Soviet Union. At the same time, in response to changing domestic conditions evolving from comparative liberalism to repression, the Japanese Communist Party transformed itself. In the 1920's much of the iceberg of the Party structure was visible, auxiliary front organizations were assigned a major role, and Party members participated rather actively in the political and cultural life of the country, displaying a relatively democratic outlook and dealing with Japanese reality. In the period of repression, the Party became a narrow organization of conspirators who were as much concerned with protecting their organization as with reaching out to other groups, and who thus were increasingly isolated from their national environment. It is this latter experience, reinforced by the years of prison or exile shared by virtually all current JCP leaders, that has left its mark on Japanese Communist Party leadership and has long made it difficult for them to adapt to the wholly different conditions—legality of Communist activity and a weakening of domestic resistance to communism—which now prevail in Japan.

2: Postwar Role and Organization

Postwar Japan ranks among the world's technologically most advanced nations. But the rate of economic growth and technological change has been so rapid that the transformation of the country's social and economic institutions has lagged behind. Japan's economy has developed unevenly; familiar social patterns of organization, such as the family system, have been weakened or destroyed by wide-ranging, liberalizing reforms; and the traditional value system has been seriously eroded but new standards have not yet taken its place. Inevitably, in the present state of flux, this society exhibits certain weaknesses and tensions which permit exploitation by political opposition groups. The Japanese Communist Party (JCP), a legal institution since 1945, plays such an adversary role in a context of maximum democratic freedom.

In other Asian countries, the Communists are not merely critics of the existing system but also function as catalysts of modernization in fighting to eliminate antiquated political and economic institutions. In Japan, however, in many respects the government itself has pre-empted this function. Nor can the JCP feed on the unfulfilled aspirations and ambitions of individuals or groups frustrated by a lack of opportunity to apply their training and education, for there is no unemployment of skilled labor or highly trained intellectual talent in contemporary Japan. In fact, Japanese society provides increasingly abundant opportunities for social mobility in an ever-expanding economy. Conditions in postwar Japan therefore do not generally favor the Communists.

It must also be noted that as protester against the existing social and political order, the JCP is not without rivals, for there are several opposition parties which seek to revamp that system. Even as a political force aimed at revolutionary change along Marxist lines, the Party is not unique in Japan, for it must compete with a long-established and radical Socialist party which agitates for the creation of a socialist order built on Marxist theory.

Although the Japanese Communist Party is today the largest non-ruling Communist party outside Western Europe, its strength at the

TABLE 1. *JCP Fortunes in House of Representatives Elections*

Year	JCP Vote		Seats Won (total=467 to 486)	
	Number (thousands)	% of vote cast	Number	% of total
1955	733	2.0	2	0.4
1958	1,012	2.6	1	0.2
1960	1,157	2.9	3	0.6
1963	1,646	4.0	5	1.1
1967	2,191	4.8	5	1.1
1969	3,199	6.8	14	2.9

TABLE 2. *JCP Fortunes in House of Councillors Elections*

Year	JCP Vote		Seats Won
	Number (thousands)	% of vote cast	(total= 250 to 252)
1956 n*	599	2.1	1
p†	1,149	3.9	1
Total			2
1959 n	552	1.9	1
p	999	3.3	0
			1
1962 n	1,124	3.1	2
p	1,760	4.8	1
			3
1965 n	1,652	4.4	2
p	2,609	6.9	2
			4
1968 n	2,147	5.0	5
p	3,577	8.3	2
			7
1971 n	3,219	8.1	8
p	4,879	12.0	2
			10

n* = *national constituency*
p† = *prefectural constituency*

polls remains insufficient to provide it with much parliamentary political leverage. Even so, the Party is not without influence in Japan. It can draw on strong support and sympathy among the influential Japanese intelligentsia and has a firm base in their professional and cultural organizations; it also wields some influence within labor unions and within special groups, primarily anti-U.S. base and peace movements; and it finds temporary or local alliances with the Socialist opposition mainstream to be feasible and often politically effective. Moreover, the Party's leverage is enhanced by its superior organization and by the discipline that makes many of its members respond to calls for intensive participation in the political struggle, something other Japanese political parties find difficult to do.

A good yardstick for the numerical strength of the JCP is the results of national elections during the past decade. (One must take into account, however, that the Japanese electoral system is not strictly proportional and tends to favor the larger parties, particularly the ruling party; that the results are strongly influenced by personalities and, on the local level at least, by issues of parochial rather than national significance; and, finally, that in the case of the minor parties success or failure may depend very much on their ability to pool votes with other organizations through promoting a single candidate.)

On the basis of the electoral figures for the past decade, it is estimated that somewhere between 5 percent and 10 percent of the adult population of Japan supports the JCP, with the percentage showing a gradual but steady increase. Support for the Party is generally much larger in the major urban centers, where it averages 10 percent and goes in some instances as high as 30 percent.*

The Party's resort to Molotov cocktails and violence prior to 1955 proved counterproductive. During the past decade, therefore, the JCP has abandoned revolutionary violence as a preferred strategy. It now assumes a posture which, while vocally militant, is nonviolent in practice and concentrates on down-to-earth issues and work at the grass-roots level. For these and other reaspons, the Party has come to enjoy increasing tolerance within Japanese society, almost approaching the condition of the French and Italian Communist parties. The Japanese

---

*In the House of Councillors elections of 1968, the highest percentages of Communist votes were cast (in descending order) in Kyoto, Tokyo, Osaka, Nagano, Kanagawa (Yokohama), and Fukuoka.

Communists are socially and politically no longer isolated as they were in prewar days. Membership in the organization does not automatically bar one from a position of influence in society, nor is it considered incompatible with teaching or other positions funded by the government. Today, the Party is viewed by many Japanese as a potential member of an alliance of "progressive forces."

On the surface at least, the Japanese Communist Party appears to have moved toward accommodation with a democratic system. But the Party's leadership remains rather dogmatic and rigid. Such rigidity is reflected in an organizational setup that has changed little over the last decade and in the insistence that the Party member stray not an iota from the official Party line. Even in these matters, however, a trend is visible which if unchecked will bring about changes in orientation. With the influx of new, young members lacking prewar or wartime experience and with their gradual rise to positions of influence within the Party apparatus, a slow transformation is taking place. This portends a gradual broadening of the Party elite, greater receptivity to pragmatic approaches, and generally more stress on independent thinking, irrespective of advice proffered from abroad.

During the past decade the Communists have made some progress toward integrating themselves into the Japanese political environment, at some detriment to the revolutionary momentum of earlier days. Even though the Party's July 1969 pledge that it would not outlaw other parties should it come to power as a member of a "dictatorship of people's democratic forces" need not be taken at face value, it is significant that the Party leadership was willing to make such a statement and that this expression of "revisionist attitudes" caused hardly a ripple among the Party members.

PARTY MEMBERSHIP

Although, as in the past, a few clandestine Party members may exist in the Japanese Communist apparatus and would not figure in the officially announced total of Party membership, their number is likely to have dwindled to a negligible figure[1] as the JCP turned, in the early 1950's, to a strategy of open political struggle. Moreover, legal reporting requirements for political organizations in Japan are quite stringent and the Japanese security agencies are very alert. At any rate,

Japanese government authorities who supervise such organizations accept the figures reported by the JCP as essentially correct.*

During the past decade JCP membership has rather steadily grown, as suggested by Table 3, which is based on data from official Party publications and from Japanese government White Papers and similar reports.

TABLE 3. *JCP Membership*

Year	Number
July 1958 (7th Party Congress)	45,000
July 1961 (8th Party Congress)	88,000
November 1964 (9th Party Congress)	140,000
November 1965	165,000
October 1966 (10th Party Congress)	250-270,000
July 1970 (11th Party Congress)	300,000

After having declined somewhat in the winter of 1967 and the spring of 1968 (due to dissension caused by the Sino-Soviet conflict), current Party membership has reached the historical peak of 300,000. While this figure represents less than 1 percent of the adult population of Japan, it places the JCP organization ahead of the Japan Socialist Party, which commands much larger electoral support.

JCP members have become progressively younger: the majority of new members in the past five years have come from the eighteen-to-thirty age bracket, many from the Communist auxiliary, the Democratic Youth League, comprising students and youth groups. Authoritative Japanese sources estimate that of the 300,000 officially reported

*Authoritative Japanese Government sources, however, make a distinction between "Party membership reported" and "actual membership," which is estimated at 20 percent less than the reported figures. The Party itself admits that roughly that percentage of its members fail to pay dues, attend Party meetings, or otherwise participate in Party affairs without having cancelled their affiliation with the JCP. In the mid-1960's the percentage of membership dilution may have run even higher due to the sudden massive increase of members and the resultant lowering of general discipline. The most recently announced figure of "about 300,000" may be fairly close to the actual membership, since the Party during 1969 sought to stress quality over quantity.

Party members, roughly one half now belong to this age bracket. One indicator of the increasing youthfulness of the Party is the growth of the Democratic Youth League itself, which is the principal source of new Party members. In 1961, it had 60,000 members, of whom 18,000 were reported to have belonged to the Party. In 1966, these figures had grown to 200,000 and 60,000 respectively. A Japanese government White Paper put the total membership at 210,000 in late 1969, including 16,000 "activists."

Only fragmentary data are available regarding the number of women in the JCP. However, it is known that their percentage has recently risen as a result of greater emphasis on building up auxiliary women's fronts and on inducing women active in the peace movement to join Party ranks. Thus, at the 1967 festival of the Party organ *Akahata,* housewives (and children) constituted as high as 25 percent of the attendance. A variety of indicators suggest that the percentage of women members in the Party is now about 10 to 15 percent. This trend is confirmed by the fact that the New Japan Women's Society, which is under Party control, had 34,000 members in 1961 (of whom 5,000 were also Party members), while the latest corresponding figures (1966) show 90,000 and 18,000, respectively. (Data on the marital status of the membership are not available, nor is information on religious distribution, which at any rate plays at most a subordinate role in Japan.) Virtually no data have been published regarding the educational level of Party members, except for the leadership. Some idea can be gained, however, from the social composition of the rank and file (see below), which suggests that while Party members are of course literate—as is virtually the entire Japanese population—an educational attainment below college predominates except in the case of Party leaders and the intellectuals. The latter, however, make up a comparatively large portion of the Party membership as well as of Party sympathizers.

As might be expected, membership is distributed quite unevenly throughout the country. By the Party's own admission,[2] this long-standing imbalance has been further aggravated during the past several years by an influx of new members from the more industrialized areas of Japan, where conditions generally favor JCP membership campaigns and where the Party has long had a much better-developed organizational apparatus than in the countryside. In 1956, official statistics estimated that more than half of the total Party membership were located in the six largest Japanese cities; this distributive pattern favoring the big cities has become somewhat more pronounced during the past decade. Generally speaking, JCP membership is highest in the principal industrial centers, lower in mixed industrial-rural areas, and lowest in the purely agricultural regions.*

The JCP publishes only figures relative to the ratio of Party members to eligible voters in the various prefectures rather than the number of Party members for each prefecture (which doubles as the basic electoral district). Such data confirm the above assessment, which is also borne out by an analysis of the electoral results of the past decade, although there are some exceptions to the general rule of JCP geographic distribution. The Party states that as of late 1966 it did best in the ratio of Party members to eligible voters in Japan's most heavily industrialized and intellectual center, the Tokyo Metropolitan district. A few years ago, Kyoto, a city of small crafts and many intellectuals, outranked Tokyo, although today it may again be in second place. In third position is Fukuoka Prefecture, known for its ailing mining industry and for its high rate of unemployment, as well as for the presence there of a major (recently deactivated) U.S. air base. But in fourth place is Nagano Prefecture, which has some industry but is predominantly agricultural. Its strong support for the JCP may be largely due to its long-standing tradition of radicalism, which affects even many of Nagano's rural districts. Nagano is followed by Kōchi Prefecture, which is characterized by sharp ultraconservative/radical leftist polarization.

Some measure of the relative Communist influence in urban versus rural areas can also be obtained by studying the results of local elections. In Tokyo in 1969 the JCP gained 18 seats out of a total of 126 and increased its proportion of the total vote to 14.4 percent. On the other hand, in the rural areas, Communist candidates often cannot garner more than 1 or 2 percent of the vote. By 1969 the JCP had been able to place 1,600 Assemblymen in Japan's prefectural, city, and town assemblies. In 80 of the country's 564 cities the mayor had been elected with Communist support. (One of these was a card-carrying Party member and 16 others had run on a coalition ticket sponsored by the JCP and one or several other parties.) The most important of these

*Analyzing the results of the national elections of December 27, 1969, the *Asahi Shimbun* of December 29, 1969, tabulated JCP strength in the elections as follows: (1) big cities (32 electoral districts)–11.6%; (2) towns (18)–6.3%; (3) semi-urban areas (53)–4%; (4) rural areas (20)–4.5%. (Interestingly, the Kōmeitō showed a very similar distributive pattern, with 17.4%, 11.0%, 6.9%, and 7.5%, respectively.)

cases were those of Tokyo governor Minobe Ryōkichi, and Kyoto governor Ninagawa Torazō, both of them non-Communists, who had the support of the JCP. Currently, the JCP is represented in roughly 75 percent (422 out of 564) of the municipal assemblies of Japan, but in only 24 percent (1,980 out of 2,716) of those in the smaller towns and villages. Analysis of election results district by district also appears to confirm this distributional ratio.

The influence of personalities and local issues (such as problems caused by U.S. air bases) further complicates an analysis of the reasons for the geographic pattern of Communist strength in Japan. On the basis of the available evidence, however, it can be concluded that Communist strength tends to be greatest when one or a combination of the following factors are present: (1) a high and rapid rate of industrialization producing substantial social instability, (2) the presence of a semi-feudal power structure that is being challenged by newly rising elements, (3) local problems to which the authorities cannot provide an immediate solution, and (4) a tradition of radicalism.

Structure

Leadership. The legal apparatus of the JCP is organized much like that of other Communist parties in the developed part of the world. Although before 1955 the JCP had a well-developed underground organization, there is no indication that any but officially acknowledged Party leaders have decision-making power in the JCP today, and these men have long been satisfactorily identified. For analytical purposes, therefore, it will suffice to examine those Party officials who are members of the higher levels of the Party hierarchy and the middle-level cadres from whom the leaders' successors have in the past invariably been recruited.

The official Communist report of the Tenth Party Congress,* held in October 1966, provides data on 1,000 Congress delegates, conveying some idea of the composition of the JCP cadres. According to that document, 94 percent of the delegates were men, 6 percent women. The age group under twenty-five constituted only 4 percent of the total; 27 percent were in the twenty-six to thirty-five age bracket; 49 percent between thirty-six and forty-five; 10 percent between forty-six and fifty-five; and 10 percent over fifty-six. As to length of Party

*The often-announced and much-postponed Eleventh Party Congress finally convened in early July 1970.

service, 1.2 percent had served less than two years; 7.6 percent had belonged to the Party for two to five years; 17.6 percent between five and ten years; and the remainder more than ten years. Roughly one fourth of the Party delegates were products of the post-Stalin era and more than 70 percent of the cadres had been in the Party for more than a decade.

With respect to social background, the delegate profile shows 47.5 percent industrial and other "actual" workers; 29.5 percent workers in white-collar positions; 2.7 percent farmers classified as "poor" and 2.6 percent farmers described as "middle"; 6 percent "working citizens" (presumably mostly women); 10 percent intellectuals; 1.7 percent others.

No recent satisfactory breakdown of the background of the highest Party cadres, the members of the Central Committee, is available. The latest pertinent information is for 1962. No major shifts appear to have basically modified these data. According to an authoritative Japanese government White Paper, the Party's Central Committee members at the time listed their professional background as follows: workers, 32 percent; public service employees, 20.4 percent; school teachers, 4.9 percent; students, 9.7 percent; farmers and fishermen, 1.9 percent; office employees of companies and shops, 14.6 percent; professional people, 10.7 percent; newspaper reporters, 3.9 percent; others, 1.9 percent.

Some idea of the leaders' educational background suggestive of the important role intellectuals play at the highest Party level can be obtained from Japanese biographical reference works, which list about three-fourths of the current Central Committee members. Though 20 members are unaccounted for (presumably they are new figures without much of a public record), the remaining 68 can be classified as follows: 24 have a university education (all but 3 graduated); 22 went to junior college or to higher professional schools (6 did not complete the course, probably owing to political persecution); 5 went to teachers' normal schools (2 dropped out before graduation); 2 went to old-style middle schools corresponding to U.S. high schools (one left before graduation); 9 completed junior high school; 5 went only to primary school; and one is a graduate of the Harbin Institute (in formerly Japanese-controlled Manchuria), and thus would rank close to the university graduate group.

The average age of Central Committee (CC) members in 1969 was fifty-eight, and the median age between fifty-nine and sixty. How great the influence of old-timers remains is indicated in age distribution: only four men are still—and just barely—in their thirties, while the same number are between seventy and eighty, and 22 are in their sixties. This rather surprising image of a revolutionary party directed by old men of prewar vintage is even more pronounced in the composition of the most powerful Party committee, the Central Committee's Presidium, whose members averaged fifty-nine years of age when they were elected in 1966. Presidium candidate members were only slightly younger. Modest attempts were made in 1966 to introduce new blood into the upper Party levels. But true to the traditional Japanese emphasis on seniority, the new appointments have done little to give the JCP a fresh young look: newly elected Central Committee members averaged forty-seven years; the re-elected CC candidate members were on the average forty-five, and their new colleagues only one year younger. At future Party congresses some attempt no doubt will be made to give the Party leadership a younger image, but it seems unlikely even then that the grip of the older men on the levers of command will be rapidly weakened.*

An analysis of the origin of new Central Committee members shows no particular pattern. This would suggest that in the rise of a Party member to cadre status and higher, ties created by common regional origin are no longer a major factor—rather a departure from the usual Japanese success model, wherein a leader-follower relationship based on common geographic origin is significant in determining success or failure in politics. Conclusions derived from the foregoing data are further corroborated by a more detailed examination of the background and careers of the top Party leadership.[3]

The most important Party leaders (primarily members of the Presidium and, to a lesser extent, key figures in the substantially overlapping Secretariat) are veterans of the prewar Communist movement, averaging

---

*After this text was written, the Eleventh Congress of the JCP convened in Tokyo in early July 1970. The congress expanded the Central Committee and introduced other changes bearing on Party organization while lowering only slightly the average age of the members of the leading Party committees. The average age of the new 110-member Central Committee at the time of their election was fifty-six years. (The 46 alternate members, however, were only 47.9 years on the average.) The new 31-member Presidium averages 57.2 years and the elite seven-member Standing Presidium 57.6 years. The latter figure would be substantially higher were it not for the inclusion in this group of the forty-year old Fuwa Tetsuzō, the first representative of the postwar generation to rise to prominence in the Japanese Communist movement.

among them some three decades of service to the Party. Their loyalty has been tested in the Communist underground. Psychologically, they bear the marks of ten or more years of detention and police repression or of exposure to an equally long exile in Stalinist Russia and Mao's China. The influence of those to whom Stalinism and wartime political persecution are mere abstractions is as yet hardly felt at the top level of the JCP, although this group will eventually have to replace their elders. This event may seem imminent, since Party Chairman Nosaka is approaching eighty, but those who are closer to the actual direction of Party affairs, like Secretary General Miyamoto Kenji or Presidium members Hakamada Satomi, Kasuga Shōichi, and Nishizawa Tomio, are in their fifties and sixties—young as Japanese politicians go.

Those at the very top of the Party pyramid are mostly well educated and of middle-class origin. Their biographical sketches show the names of the most respected Japanese academic institutions. Both present Secretary General Miyamoto and his rival Shiga Yoshio graduated from Tokyo (Imperial) University. Keio University, an outstanding private institution, is the alma mater of Chairman Nosaka. Top JCP leaders also have deep familiarity with life under communism abroad—in the Soviet Union and in China. Nosaka, a charter member of the British Communist Party, spent a decade in the Soviet Union as Japanese delegate to the Comintern and subsequently several years in wartime China at Communist headquarters in Yenan. Miyamoto has a substantial acquaintance with the Soviet Union. And Hakamada, one of the few Party leaders of genuinely proletarian background, received much of his education in the U.S.S.R.

In fact, it is because of long exile or imprisonment that top Party leaders' knowledge of Japanese reality is sketchy and distorted. Psychologically they may find it difficult to break out of the Stalinist mold and adjust to the vastly changed postwar environment, where even the notoriously dogmatic Japanese intellectuals are turning away from rigid positions. At this point in history, despite progress in exploiting the opportunities presented in a democratic system, the JCP remains among the more inflexible of the world's nonruling Communist parties. Moreover, its leaders tend to oppose new trends for Party democratization that are beginning to stir the lower levels of the Party hierarchy.

The JCP has long presented the paradox of an organization beset by factional struggle but whose leadership has shown a high degree of stability and continuity. In the past, factional and doctrinal disputes have generally resulted in changes in the leadership's pecking order, but they have rarely denied the loser a position of responsibility or expelled him from the Party. But the crucial issues posed by the Sino-Soviet confrontation have begun to affect even the leadership of the Japanese Communist hierarchy in recent years. The May 1964 expulsion of No. 2 man Shiga Yoshio (who supported the nuclear test ban against the dictates of the then Peking-oriented Presidium) was an unusual event in the JCP's postwar history, although lesser figures had lost their Party cards earlier for similar reasons. After 1966, when the JCP came into open conflict with Mao's China, some middle-level leaders were purged but the top leadership survived virtually intact.*

*Although the Eleventh Party Congress of July 1970 brought some new faces into leading Party committees, the hierarchy at the top still is composed almost exclusively of prewar Communists. A striking exception is Fuwa Tetsuzō (pseudonym of Ueda Kenjirō, whose older brother Kōichirō is also a Presidium member), protégé of Miyamoto Kenji.

The youthful Fuwa (born in 1930) is a member of the postwar generation of Japanese Communists, but by the time of his elevation to Standing Presidium membership he had accumulated more than two decades of Party experience. He joined the JCP in 1947 while still a student in Tokyo's elite First Higher School. At Tokyo University, Japan's most prestigious academic institution, Fuwa chose the difficult course of the natural sciences; he graduated with a degree in physics in 1953. Thereafter he made labor-union activity his career until 1964, when he was invited to work at Party headquarters. There he specialized in Marxist-Leninist theory and international problems. In 1964 he was also made a candidate (alternate) member of the Party's Central Committee, and two years later, he became a full member of that body. In 1966 he was a member of an important Party mission to North Vietnam, Communist China, and North Korea. He has written numerous articles and many authoritative Party statements on international problems and on right and left wing ideological deviations from the Party line. His importance in the movement is further reflected in the fact that he is one of the few JCP leaders whose writings have been issued in book form for the general public. Clearly, Fuwa is considered by the Party elders to be one of the most promising if not *the* most promising of the younger Communists. Perhaps the fact that he is the only Standing Presidium member to hold a seat in the Diet has also helped to speed up Fuwa's advancement to the highest level of the Party hierarchy.

Although the seventy-eight-year-old Nosaka Sanzō remains Chairman of the Central Committee and thus Party Chairman, his role in the Party is now largely a symbolic one. This is reflected in the fact that he no longer is a member even of the Presidium, which since the Eleventh Congress is headed by Miyamoto Kenji, the de facto leader of the Party. The JCP no longer has a Secretary General (Miyamoto's former title). Instead, the new post of Chief of the Party Secretariat was created and filled by Fuwa Tetsuzō. This position wields substantially less influence and enjoys less prestige than that of the Presidium Chairman, on whom it is at any rate dependent: under the new arrangement the Presidium and not the Central Committee appoints the members of the Secretariat.

Rank and File. The most recent comprehensive data on the social origins and professional backgrounds of the rank and file come from a 1962 percentage breakdown:[4]

```
Professional Party members ........................2.15%
Factory workers ...............................13.58
General workers (small
    and medium enterprises) ......................10.51
Laborers .....................................5.27
Public service employees .........................12.75
Teachers ....................................6.64
Workers in agriculture,
    forestry, fishing ...........................11.35
Office workers ................................9.25
Dealers and merchants ...........................7.20
Company managers .............................0.76
Liberal professions ............................4.26
Others ......................................3.66
No regular occupation ..........................4.55
Unknown ...................................6.52
```

A White Paper on Japanese communism issued by the Japanese government in 1967 reported that at the time of the Tenth Congress (1966) roughly 162,500 of the 250,000 active members belonged to the various "worker" categories, which thus constituted more than 65 percent of the total membership. This same source indicated that an earlier trend had continued unabated, thus changing the membership makeup by lowering the average age of the Party members and reducing the average period of their Party experience, and by increasing the relative weights of the working class and women within Party ranks.

The same report analyzed the age distribution of a sample region in 1966: 12 percent of new Party members were eighteen or nineteen years old (eighteen is the minimum age for admission to the Party); 69 percent were between twenty and twenty-four; 13 percent were between twenty-five and twenty-nine; and only 6 percent were over thirty. Classified by profession, new members were 32 percent workers, 46 percent general and clerical workers, 12 percent students, and 10 percent farmers, self-employed, and other.* In light of the current

---

*The author's examination of a variety of available Japanese sources produced the following conclusion about the approximate social and professional distribution of the Party membership in mid-1968: factory workers, 16%; clerical workers, 14%; other workers, 11%; government employees (excluding teachers), 17%; teachers, 7%; students, 1%; farmers, 8%; business and professions, 10%; unemployed, 6%; miscellaneous, 10%.

composition of the Party rank and file, a typical JCP member would be a young man with less than five years of membership—quite in contrast to the cadres and the leadership—and belonging to the working class (defined broadly to include clerical workers in government services and corporations). The membership remains above the Japanese average in educational attainment, although the level is not as high as a few years ago when nearly 15 percent of Party members were university graduates and another 25 percent could claim high school graduation.

Significantly, many of the JCP rank and file are Japanese government employees. In late 1966, they totaled 48,000, about 20 percent of the total Party membership. Their distribution within the government services was then as follows:

Government administrative organs
  (including postal services) 9,300
Public corporations 1,700
Government schools (teachers) 15,000
Public enterprises (railroads,
  electric power) 11,000
Local government organizations 11,000

Another characteristic of the JCP membership is its heavy concentration in the strategic sectors of private industry, particularly in mass communications and transportation. Figures for late 1966 indicate the following distribution:

Mining and steel industry 8,000
Machine-building 11,500
Chemical industry 5,000
Financial institutions and
  insurance companies 3,000
Mass media and printing 6,500
Shipbuilding 2,200
Textiles 2,600
Transportation 6,000
Electricity, gas 2,200

Respect for authority and a willingness to subordinate oneself to superiors has long been a characteristic of members of Japanese society. It has thus been relatively easy for the average JCP member to accept the guidance of his seniors. But this responsiveness to established leadership is diminishing in postwar Japan from the influence of an open and extremely permissive society, which allows the individual to challenge all authority and confronts him with diverse viewpoints while offering opportunities to resist authority. This breakdown of the old order, which has occurred in the JCP as in other sectors of Japanese life, has been accelerated by a generation gap that has developed between the leadership, formed in prewar autocratic traditions, and the majority of young Party members, who have known neither Stalinism nor the police regime of pre-surrender Japan.

Anti-authoritarian sentiments accumulated under the surface during the first postwar decade of the Party's legal existence. During the second decade they have been catalyzed by the open feuds over strategy set off among the leadership by the Sino-Soviet controversy. These disagreements have resulted in frequent changes of policy and, worse yet, in contradictory Party positions that have weakened respect for the leaders' authority. The rapid influx of new and mostly young members, products of a free and liberal postwar society, has further aggravated the Party's discipline problem.

This is reflected in the rising number of card-carrying members who refuse or passively resist participation in Party-ordained training sessions or similar functions, in their laxity about paying Party dues, in their often unenthusiastic response to Party campaigns, and generally in a lowering of the level of what is termed "Party spirit and Party consciousness." It is difficult to assign numerical weight to these phenomena, but frequent Party complaints indicate the seriousness with which the JCP views these trends. The Party reported with dismay, for example, that a major Party rally scheduled in late 1966 to gather 200,000 members and sympathizers met only 30 percent of this goal, largely because of insufficient response from the rank and file rather than a lack of cadre effort. Illustrating the Party's problem with even some of its lower cadres, the official Party daily pointed out that a most important editorial which the Central Committee had made required reading was not being studied by the Party cell chiefs as promptly as had been demanded. It was reported that in a sample area of northern Japan only 24 percent had read about half of the document; 24 percent replied that they had "just got started"; and 22 percent hadn't got around to it at all.

Relaxation of Party discipline currently appears to be no more than an incipient trend, but the JCP is fully aware of its dangers. Especially since 1968, the Party has intensified attempts to correct this, primarily by revitalizing the organization through imposing tighter controls and reshuffling cadres and by increasing training and indoctrination courses for Party members. This program involves special classes for women, and rural and youth activities and efforts to regularize meeting schedules for the various Party organizations, from prefectural Party assemblies down to district assemblies and cells. More difficult to combat than the general trend toward laxity is the active dissidence among the more radical, activist members generated by the JCP's recent shift away from endorsing Maoist policies. A few entire Party units have broken away from the direction of the Center and with Chinese Communist assistance are trying further to subvert the Party apparatus and discipline. The JCP Center has reacted by initiating a massive anti-Maoist campaign within the Party and by imposing restrictions on members' travel to Communist China.

Distribution of Supporters. The pattern of distribution of JCP supporters—i.e., members and sympathizers—has been discussed previously in examining Communist electoral support. The organizational means by which the Party mobilizes such backing at the polls and in the streets, as well as the underlying causes for Party support, are analyzed in a later chapter on JCP strategy past and present. The following data may serve to supplement the picture.

Currently the JCP is sufficiently popular in at least three of the four major industrial regions of Japan—Tokyo, Osaka, and Fukuoka—to have elected a representative to the Lower House from these districts. In addition, it has been successful in the Kyoto, Kōchi, and Nagano areas, where conditions are particularly favorable, as noted above. The Tokyo and Kyoto regions have also sent Communists to the Upper House (Chairman Nosaka is the Tokyo representative), attesting again to the strong Party position there. A statistical table published by the Party organ *Akahata* after the 1968 House of Councillors elections confirms that the JCP finds its strongest support in the industrial areas, but has made much less headway in most rural districts, mainly because of the continued hold of traditional conservative leadership over the Japanese village and the postwar solution of the tenant labor/poor farmer problem through nationwide land reform.

No precise figures are available regarding the percentage of major population groups that support the Communist Party. There is general agreement, however, that the rank order of support for the JCP runs from intellectuals (particularly social scientists and students) to workers in government agencies and corporations, disadvantaged workers in small and medium enterprises, workers in private industry, the farming population, and the self-employed in nonintellectual professions.

Formal Organization Versus Actual Performance. The JCP's formal organization does not differ in essentials from that of its counterparts in other developed countries where Communist parties operate legally. At the top of the hierarchy is the Central Committee, elected by the Party Congress, with its leading inner core, the Presidium. Party hierarchy then runs, in descending order, to 46 prefectural committees, 239 district committees, and approximately (in 1966) 13,000 cells (14,000 in 1968).*

The distribution of these cells as last officially reported (late 1966) provides clues to the sources of Communist strength in Japan and the relative effectiveness of the JCP in various sectors of Japanese life. This distribution has probably changed little since, and is as follows:

> 3,200 cells in governmental organizations
> 4,000 in private enterprises
> 2,900 in residential districts
> 1,500 in agricultural communities
> 1,400 in various other categories of organization.†

It is noteworthy that during the 1960's the last three categories increased numerically only 20 to 80 percent, while the two first

*The Eleventh Party Congress adopted a new set of Party regulations which clearly reflects the trend toward adaptation to the Japanese environment and the Party's desire to create the image of an organization that operates independently of foreign influence and in the national interest. The preamble of the document stresses the need for "independent and creative development of the theory and practice of the Japanese revolution"; speaks of "holding fast to the position of autonomy and independence combining proletarian internationalism and true patriotism"; and declares that the Party will resolutely fight any intereference in its affairs by "great-power chauvinism." In line with the desired more democratic image, the new Party regulations avoid use of the traditional term "Party cell" with its conspiratorial flavor and employ instead the terms "basic organization" or "branch," terms which are being used also by other Japanese political parties. (Quotations translated from the official Japanese text as published in the Party publication *Gekkan Gakushū* (Monthly Study), August 1970, pp. 135-47). Also, for the first time in Party history, the JCP congress held all its sessions in public except those meetings concerned with financial and personnel matters.

†Unofficial but authoritative Japanese sources give the following percentages for 1968, suggesting that no shift in the distinctive pattern had occurred: government organizations, 24%; private enterprise, 33%; residential districts, 22%; agricultural communities, 11%; others, 10%.

categories increased by 400 percent each, an indication of the Party's success in strengthening its base in the two most vulnerable and at the same time most strategic sectors of the country, the government and industry.

JCP influence also reaches into a wide range of special target groups through the Party's auxiliary and front organizations. The major ones in late 1966 (more recent reliable data are unavailable), their reported total membership, and the estimated number of Party members (in parentheses) are shown below:

Japan Democratic Youth League	200,000 (60,000)
New Japan Women's Society	100,000 (20,000)
National Federation of Rural Labor Unions	20,000(2,000)
Federation of National Commercial and Industrial Organizations	90,000 (5,000)
National Federation for Protection of Life and Health	77,000 (3,000)
National Federation of Japan Democratic Medical Organizations	7,500 (2,200)
Japan Peace Committee	37,000 (13,600)
Japan Council of Scientists	5,000 (?)
Japan Democratic Literary League	2,200 (?)
New Japan Athletic Federation	10,000 (?)

Communist influence is also strong in a score of other organizations with a total membership exceeding 3 million (see chapter four).

More difficult than to describe the formal organization of the JCP and its auxiliaries is to evaluate their effectiveness—beyond the gross measurement of electoral results—and their style of operation. The JCP has always lacked a charismatic leader. The one who came closest was the late Secretary General Tokuda Kyūichi, who died in exile in Communist China in the late 1950's. Neither his associate Nosaka Sanzō, a mild-mannered, scholarly man, nor Miyamoto Kenji, nor Hakamada Satomi, nor any of their junior colleagues appear to have that certain quality which distinguishes an inspiring leader. The result—a natural response to the Japanese environment, which is characterized by bureaucratic procedures and consensus policies—has been a Japanese Communist Party that at least since the mid-fifties has been bureaucratic in its style of operations and without clearcut focus on a single authority. The leading Party group is often described as a collective leadership. More correctly, it must be characterized as an association of a few individuals who are disinclined to risk an all-out power struggle but are sufficiently ambitious to keep the Party leadership in a state of potential disequilibrium and tension. Until the Old Guard passes away it seems unlikely that the leading cadres will produce any single leader who could impose his will on the Party apparatus, although in the last several years the (in 1970) sixty-one-year-old Miyamoto Kenji has clearly established himself as primus inter pares.

We have already pointed to a certain organizational weakness in the Party caused by the dual impact of a permissive, open society and the massive influx of new, unindoctrinated members. This weakness is constantly being fought and probably prevented from further affecting Party cohesion and influence by an extremely well-developed and ably managed communications apparatus which, in turn, reflects one of modern Japan's greatest strengths.

The Communist Party's press and communications network is efficiently run and reaches well beyond the larger urban centers. Allowing for a certain inflation (perhaps 10 percent) in JCP-reported circulation figures, the following list of selected Party publications and their circulation as of late 1969 indicates the size of the Communist communications media and their variety:

Akahata (daily Party organ) 400,000
Akahata (Sunday edition) 1,400,000
Zen'ei (theoretical monthly) 90,000
Sekai Seiji Shiryō (materials on
    international affairs) 35,000
Gikai to Jichitai (monthly reports
    on parliamentary affairs) 15,000
Gakusei Shimbun (for the student) 20,000
Minsei Shimbun (youth movement) 250,000
Gekkan Gakushū (Party education monthly) 110,000
Dokusho no tomo (book reviews) 12,000
Bunka Hyōron (cultural and literary) 15,000

Maintenance of Party discipline and the authority of the Central Committee are further strengthened by massive indoctrination drives that require many full-time professional Party workers and large funds. Both appear to be available in sufficient quantity.

The exact amount of funds the JCP raises and how is a closely guarded secret, of course, but the stringent Japanese government reporting requirements for political organizations allow us to guess from its own reports at the minimum funding level the Party commands. (This figure would not include, for obvious reasons, foreign subsidies, which reportedly have been quite substantial as long as the JCP remained in the good graces of Peking.) The JCP is fairly big business today, to judge by the size of its printing plants and the vast amount of literature it issues. Much of the Party's income presumably comes from its publishing. Whatever the sources, official statistics indicate that in 1969 the JCP's revenues, amounting to more than $9 million, exceeded those of all but the ruling Liberal Democratic Party, which receives substantial subsidies from business circles. JCP income was more than five times that of its Socialist rivals, although the latter poll several times the vote of the Communists—an indication of the relative organizational weakness of the one and the strength of the other of the two Marxist opposition parties.

What resources the Party can mobilize when it galvanizes efforts to reaffirm the Center's authority over the rank and file can be surmised from a recent episode. When the JCP's decision to reject Maoist policy positions created dissension in Communist ranks, the Central Committee decided to launch an intensive propaganda drive to enlighten the confused Party membership. In the six weeks between late October and early December 1967, Party leaders addressed 34 audiences throughout Japan, each time assembling groups of at least 300 and often more than 1,000 Party members. At the same time, the Party Secretariat and its Propaganda and Education Section poured out a flow of directives and literature explaining the Center's position to the rank and file. The Party apparatus is now sufficiently large and efficiently organized to be able to saturate the Japanese public with the Communist viewpoint by using the Party's well-developed distribution network.

How effective has the JCP been during its more than two decades of legal existence in translating aspirations into actual results? Certainly by 1970 the Party had not attained a pivotal position from which it could directly influence Japan's domestic and foreign policies or threaten the predominant position of the ruling conservative party. On the other hand, the Communist Party has succeeded in making the transition from a small, extra-legal, secret organization to a mass organization with a substantial following. The JCP has, so to speak, become part of the Japanese political scene. Whether it can develop beyond these modest attainments will depend on many factors, not the least being its ability to adapt successfully to its national environment, something it had failed to do in prewar times.

3: The JCP's National Environment

Although it is only the size of California, Japan has 100 million people, most of them compressed into a small portion of the mountainous country, particularly along the coast, where all industry is concentrated. Postwar Japan is among the world's most industrialized countries. In this, as in many other respects, Japan is an exception in Asia.

Among the world's great nations Japan probably is the least blessed with natural resources, which—with the exception of food—must come almost entirely from abroad. But the Japanese have made the most of their greatest asset, their human resources: the educational level of the Japanese people is among the world's highest; they have rightly been called "the most achievement-minded nation" and they distinguish themselves by astounding vitality and industriousness. Thus, once the rebuilding of the war-shattered economy was completed with U.S. help two decades ago, the country began to show an unprecedentedly rapid economic growth and an equally rapid rise in the standard of living. By 1970, the gross national product of Japan exceeded $170 billion, with annual per capita income well over $1,000—very high by Asian standards. Although this places Japan in the No. 3 world position in terms of total output (after the United States and the Soviet Union and substantially ahead of West Germany), the Japanese still rank only eighteenth in per capita income. This fact conveys some idea of the distance Japan will have to go before its standard of living can match that of the developed Western European nations.

In the postwar period, conditions on the whole have not favored social protest movements like the Communist Party. Japan has not only been highly successful in developing its economy and in raising its standard of living; it has also moved to adjust its political and social institutions to the modern age, away from prewar autocratic and restrictive patterns. This evolution has moderated the sharp social tensions which otherwise would have resulted from the rapidity of social change.

37

Japan is strategically the most valuable country in non-Communist Asia, and both Communist and non-Communist nations treat it accordingly. Even though economic, social, and political conditions have not been favorable to the Communists, and though the U.S. position in Japan remains strong, Moscow and Peking have continued efforts to affect Japanese policy. To influence their natural allies, the JCP, they have furnished funds, have provided ideological and operational advice, and have trained personnel. Japan's insular situation, however, hinders continuous close communication between the Communist nations on the continent and their supporters in Japan.

THE SOCIAL SYSTEM

Postwar Japan's rate of industrialization and urbanization is the fastest of the world's larger nations. The urban population now constitutes the vast majority of the total population, although the Japanese manage even today to produce the bulk of their own basic food requirements. Meanwhile the rural areas are steadily being drained of manpower; and that manpower is pouring into the expanding cities where it constitutes a source of potential unrest.

Rapid urbanization has weakened or destroyed much of the traditional social order, and Japanese society today is characterized by flux and a search for new models and patterns. Family ties and paternal authority—on which Japan's social stability has rested in the past—have been attenuated. Japan's great cities harbor millions of people of rural origin who are no longer part of rural society nor are yet at home in modern society. Feeling lost and alienated, they are attracted by any political movement that tenders definite goals and standards of behavior as passkeys to integration into a larger, stable group.

Important postwar modifications of Japan's political system (destruction of the Emperor system and the military apparatus, for example) have left many Japanese with a feeling of vague dissatisfaction, since no new purpose or national objectives have fully replaced the old ones that focused on great-power status and an "Asian mission." The JCP attempts to exploit this ideological void, but it is not the only political party to do so. It must compete with the Marxist Japanese Socialist Party and with the Kōmeitō Party, an organization with nationalist and religious underpinnings (see chapter four).

Prewar Japan was characterized by a class structure rooted in long-standing historic traditions. Postwar legal reforms have abolished such distinctions. In practice also a process of social leveling is taking place, as the middle class fuses with the upper stratum of the industrial labor force. Underprivileged social groups remain—unskilled labor and poor farmers—but they are being absorbed into the growing economy. Thus, like other advanced industrialized nations, Japan is moving away from sharp class confrontation, contrary to the prediction of Marxist theory.

The JCP has found it difficult to adjust to the reality of an evolution away from the pattern Marx considered inevitable. Prisoner of the past, the Party leadership continues—somewhat uneasily, it is true—to argue in outmoded terms of Marxist orthodoxy. Only a minority group (mostly those purged from the leadership) and the lower and younger Communist cadres show a tendency to reexamine Marxist premises in light of postwar Japanese reality.

Contrary to virtually every other country of Asia, the Japanese are ethnically homogeneous. Only two minorities exist, one of foreign and the other of predominantly Japanese origin. The first, the Korean minority, numbers about 600,000 and consists largely of the remnants of unskilled laborers who were brought to Japan, often by force, prior to and during the Second World War. Koreans are still discriminated against and tend to be ostracized by their Japanese hosts. The Japanese Communist movement has always allied with the Korean Communist movement and with left-wing Koreans residing in Japan. The JCP remains the only Japanese political party that has intimate organizational ties with the Korean minority and draws strong support from it.

The other minority group, once called *eta* (meaning "outcast" but translating literally into a much more objectionable term), are now generally referred to as "people of the special village communities," since many of them still seem to be confined to separate communities or ghetto-like parts of major towns, especially in western Japan. They number about one million. Their origin is not clear, although they are thought to descend from prisoners taken in wars with Korea at the dawn of the Japanese nation; persons ostracized for transgressing certain religious (Buddhist) and social taboos (such as the killing of animals); and people who fell—through crime or misfortune—from their class during the feudal age. Statistical data on this minority are difficult to come by since in theory they no longer exist, having been legally integrated into Japanese society. There is evidence that many of them protest their condition by supporting anti-Establishment organizations such as the JCP, which has long led the fight against social discrimination. (The strong Communist showing in Kyoto, for example, may in part relate to such support.) But this minority cannot automatically be counted as a Communist asset, for some of its most prominent leaders have traditionally associated with the radical left wing of the rival Socialist party and clashes have occurred between representatives of this minority group and the Japanese Communist Party.*

BELIEF SYSTEM

Although most Japanese belong to one or another of the many Buddhist sects in Japan, religious influence on ideology and politics until recently has been quite limited. Religion, whether in its Buddhist form or as "Shintoism" (a term used to cover the native Japanese beliefs, which in many cases have combined with Buddhism or coexist with it), is for most Japanese a matter of form rather than of substance. Japanese political thinking is thus little affected by religious beliefs except for the minority of Japanese to whom Buddhism or newer popular religious beliefs are a central living force in their lives. Hence in contemporary Japan religion poses no major obstacle to the influence and spread of communism. With the notable exception of the Sōkagakkai Buddhist movement, which has as a political arm the Kōmeitō Party, religion and politics operate in different spheres and there is little interaction. In practice, the Japanese Buddhist sects tend to favor conservative forces in society and politics and to oppose Marxism and communism. However, such opposition is on the whole a passive one and there are few open clashes between religious forces (again excepting the Kōmeitō) and the Communist movement.

Such terms as "imperialism" and "anti-imperialism" constitute part of the intellectual baggage of most modern Japanese. These terms are used frequently, and their validity is generally accepted even by those who do not subscribe to Marxist theory in toto. They are applied

---

*Such friction arises in most cases from the JCP's unwillingness to recognize the grievances of the minority group except as *one* aspect of what it terms "capitalist exploitation."

primarily in two contexts. First, it is widely assumed that prewar and wartime Japan's role in Asia was a prime example of imperialism in action, an imperialism that the Japanese associate with disastrous military defeat and immense physical and human destruction. The second, more recent context: many Japanese view the United States as "imperialistic," pointing to such aspects of U.S. policy as the postwar occupation of Japan or the American involvement in the war in Vietnam. The traditionally strong Marxist influence among Japanese intellectuals and the educated strata of society of course reinforces such interpretations of recent history. On the other hand, it must be noted that the JCP cannot hope to arouse support on the anti-imperialist theme as can other Asian Communist parties, since Japan has been spared the colonial experience of much of the rest of Asia. To most Japanese, "imperialism" connotes rather a feeling of guilt (for Japanese actions in Asia) than the bitter sentiments of Asian victims of Western "imperialism." "Imperialism" as a propaganda weapon against the United States, while no doubt potent also in Japan, is therefore not quite as effective as elsewhere in Asia.

Until its surrender to American forces, Japan had never known invasion by foreign armies, nor has it ever lost its national independence. This unusual past and the insular position of the country have minimized the fear of neighboring countries—Russia, China, and Korea—all of which, moreover, have in fact been defeated by Japanese armies at one time or another. Even today, when Japan faces a strong Soviet Union and an increasingly powerful Communist Chinese neighbor, fear of an external threat to Japan's security is not a major factor in public opinion on national defense and foreign policies. Nor is Japan beset, as are so many other Asian countries, by the fear of rebellion by a racial or other minority, since both minority groups in Japan, as pointed out earlier, are numerically too weak to present a real threat. Nor is their situation so desperate that it would drive them to direct action.

Prewar Japan was characterized by a virulent nationalism of peculiarly Japanese stamp, involving belief in the divine origin of the Imperial House, for example. World War II dealt this ultranationalism a fatal blow, however, and created the conditions for an equally powerful anti-nationalism. Confronted with the realities of international life two decades later, the Japanese are now reconsidering their role in the world. The growing economic strength of the country and a greater desire to shape Japan's policies independent of other countries, particularly the United States, have produced a new, milder, and rather non-aggressive kind of nationalism. This nationalism is directed primarily against U.S. influence in Japan's political, economic, and cultural life. Thus it tends to be associated with radical left-wing, anti-American thought. While these conditions would seem to provide the JCP with considerable assets in the political struggle, the Party, at least until recently, has been unable to ride successfully the crest of such nationalist sentiment because the Japanese Communists themselves have long had a reputation for being manipulated by foreign powers. They cannot therefore effectively act as spokesmen for Japanese nationalism. Any JCP success at playing on nationalist sentiments has been in a broad alliance with the Socialists, whose roots are more firmly planted in native soil. Nor are the Japanese Socialists the only rivals the Japanese Communists face in their attempts to monopolize the role of genuine patriots.

Anti-war sentiments are extremely powerful in contemporary Japan, owing to the Japanese people's experience with war during the 1930's and 1940's. The JCP is in a position to exploit this mood in its anti-government propaganda, for the Communists are the only ones who can point to an unblemished record of consistent opposition to Japan's foreign wars. The focus of their propaganda—the U.S.-Japanese alliance and the alleged danger of Japan's being drawn into a nuclear war—is on issues about which a great many Japanese agree and to which they respond with strong emotions. The issue of war and peace is thus a most effective one on which the Japanese Communists can attempt to build a broad popular anti-government front.

A number of other beliefs and values common to most contemporary Japanese are relevant to the JCP's effectiveness in the struggle for political power. Among those that favor the Party are a strong statist tradition in political, social, and economic matters. Transition to a socialist system in Japan therefore probably would not represent as great a departure from historic experience as it might in other developed countries. Even today, when Japan takes pride in its liberal political and economic philosophy, the government continues to play a key role in determining economic policy. This function is viewed as legitimate by most Japanese and is considered on the whole both desirable and effective.

A powerful sense of the Japanese people's "mission," which once aimed at territorial conquest and the establishment of a "new order" in Asia, is today finding an outlet in the tendency of many Japanese, particularly intellectuals and youth, to set Japan up as a model of peacefulness among the world's nations. They invoke this image to fight—"for peace," "against U.S. imperialism," against U.S. bases, and against nuclear weapons—issues which the Communists can also use against the United States and which can provide the necessary emotional thrust to launch effective mass action.

Many Japanese feel ambivalent about Japan's role in Asia and the concept of "Asianism," which draws both on Japan's Asian (i.e., Chinese) cultural heritage and on a feeling of belonging to Asia by blood and color. At the same time, they are guiltily aware that Japan is becoming less and less an Asian country as it develops into a modern, highly industrialized society resembling those of the West. Faced with this dilemma, many Japanese insist that Japan has a mission to assist Asia's modernization and must strive to develop closer ties with the Asian continent, whether that continent is Communist or not. The JCP can therefore effectively play on the theme of "friendship with all nations" and warn that alliance with America will make Japan "an orphan in Asia"—slogans which have strong emotional impact today. On the other hand, it is also true that deep down the Japanese consider themselves unique in their history, as well as in their social and political organization. The country's insular position and long isolation from events on the Asian continent have created in the Japanese subconscious a sharp "indigenous/foreign" dichotomy. Thus a party like the Communist Party, with its pronounced foreign flavor, must contend with strong suspicions and emotional antagonism as long as it cannot evoke a new image of being "genuinely Japanese."

Both in responding to crisis situations and in their attitude toward goal-achievement, the Japanese tend to be extremists: they have proven themselves capable of extreme efforts to achieve national goals. But failure to achieve such a goal—as in the case of Japan's defeat in World War II—can result in dramatic policy changes. Thus, while the Japanese people are essentially conservative toward social and political change, once the existing system fails they can initiate abrupt policy changes, although they will attempt to fit them into traditional Japanese patterns. A complete failure of the government to sustain the current momentum toward greater economic prosperity and the elimination of social inequities—unlikely as it now appears—could therefore set off powerful repercussions, which in turn might well benefit the Japanese Communists.

In contrast to prewar Japan, where all power was (in theory) vested in the divine Emperor (and in practice in a small oligarchy), postwar Japan is a constitutional monarchy in which the voter is the source of all authority. Elections provide for free expression of the popular will, and the government must command a majority in parliament (the bicameral Diet) in order to rule. Except for a very brief experiment in centrist/ moderate left coalition government in the late 1940's, postwar Japanese governments have always been in the hands of the conservatives.

Democracy as the guiding principle for political organization is widely popular in postwar Japan, although there is much criticism of the way it is being implemented by the ruling conservatives. Specific reasons for opposition to the government and the conservative Establishment include: the alleged pervasive influence of moneyed interests over policy; corruption and graft within the ruling party and their impact on policy decisions; the "dictatorship of the majority" over the weaker opposition forces, which seem forever destined to remain a minority; the allegedly heavy influence of U.S. suggestions and decisions over the policies of the Japanese government; and, generally, a feeling that after decades of conservative rule there is need for a change. However, the principal opposition party, the JSP, has proven too dogmatic, negative, and extremist in its criticism of government policy to attract sufficient popular support to oust the conservatives. Thus the Japanese electorate has always turned *faute de mieux* to the ruling Liberal Democratic Party and entrusted it with the government. This occurred most recently in late December 1969, when the conservatives won an impressive victory at the polls and crushed the opposition Socialists.

Like its many conservative predecessors, the present Satō government commands a safe majority in the Diet. The strength of the conservative camp has in the past fluctuated between two thirds and one half of the total vote, with close to one third of the electoral support going to the opposition Socialists. Recent years have witnessed a gradual erosion of electoral backing for the conservatives with several new opposition parties making their appearance and the formerly biparty political system transforming itself into a multiparty one. The last general elections (1969) may only temporarily have reversed this process of erosion of conservative power. If so, it is possible that in the coming years a restructuring of the political parties will take place. This might lead either to a coalition of the conservatives with centrist/moderate leftist forces or to the emergence of a new party composed of conservatives and centrist and perhaps moderate leftist elements. The chances of the JCP's benefiting from such developments and participating somehow in the exercise of power must, however, be rated slim.

While a change of government resulting also in modest policy changes is conceivable during the next few years, such an event is most unlikely to occur through other than democratic means. The Japanese state apparatus remains extremely strong and efficient. Its bureaucracy wields great power and distinguishes itself by competence and responsibility toward a smooth perpetuation of the existing system and the defense of Japan's national interests. It is also sufficiently innovative to adapt to new problems and situations. Further, it is intimately linked with the ruling politicians and the world of business.

Since there is also nationwide support for parliamentary government, it is not surprising that in the more than two decades since the war Japan has been free of any attempted or successful coups. Nor is it possible at this time to detect conditions within the Japanese system that could make a coup possible. Despite much publicity about Japan's new left and its groups of right-wing extremists, extremists of both right and left remain numerically weak. They lack popular support and the physical means to confront successfully the very powerful Establishment. Nor could the country's armed forces play such a role. They must operate in a climate of anti-militarism and are firmly under civilian control. For the foreseeable future no change in their subordinate policy-making position seems likely. Finally, with all its shortcomings, the present Japanese political system provides sufficient outlets for the expression of social and other grievances to obviate the conditions that would invite political change by force.

OTHER RELEVANT FACTORS

As pointed out above, the Japanese economy is not nationalized, but it is strongly influenced by the policies of the government, and its leaders are responsive to national needs as interpreted by the bureaucrats. In this sense, large and important sectors of the Japanese economy, while operating within a free-enterprise framework, are in practice close to a condition of being under state supervision. As long as the Japanese bureaucratic system retains its elasticity toward policy formulation and continues to respond to the Japanese people's social needs, it seems unlikely that conditions could develop that would encourage resort to revolutionary solutions.

The Japanese economy is also characterized by a high degree of unionization. Despite frequent strikes, the bargaining process between workers and employees on one hand and employers on the other is effective and operates with a minimum of friction. Appearances to the contrary, Japan has not experienced an all-out confrontation between labor and management that could have given rise to a revolutionary situation. Finally, it should be pointed out that acting on behalf of the strong state apparatus, the Japanese police and other security forces and agencies are well disciplined, loyal to the government in power, and extremely efficient in restraining subversive movements.

Foreign Relations: Pressures and Pulls

It is in the area of foreign relations that Japan currently experiences its most difficult challenges. Devoted to the resolution of international problems through peaceful means (Article 9 of the Constitution outlaws the use of war potential), Japan finds itself in the midst of a tense Far Eastern situation and allied to the United States, which in turn is deeply involved in military action on the Asian continent. Many Japanese disapprove of the U.S. involvement in Vietnam, as well as other aspects of U.S. policy in Asia (such as the United States' China policy). Nevertheless, under present conditions, Japan has little choice but to support the U.S. position if it is not to forego the U.S. nuclear and military umbrella.

While a substantial but shrinking portion of the Japanese public— generally identical with opposition elements—is prepared to consider various types of neutralist solutions to the Japanese international problem, the majority of the electorate does not appear to wish to take such risk. The U.S. alliance and its implications—particularly the alleged danger of Japanese military involvement with the United States— remain, however, controversial issues, which lend themselves to exploitation by domestic opposition forces as well as by Communist propaganda from abroad. These attacks are felt most acutely when they are targeted on the U.S. use of Japanese territory for military purposes, as in the maintenance of U.S. bases in Japan (including Okinawa), and in the military cooperation, even if strictly defensive, between U.S. military forces and Japan's defense establishment.

4: JCP Conflict and Integration with Its National Environment

POLITICAL STRATEGIES

Despite the numerous tactical shifts in postwar Communist strategy to seize political power in Japan, it is possible to divide the two and one-half decades since the end of the war into three major periods. These periods are distinguished by substantially differing Party approaches. In turn, they reflect the Communist leadership's changing assessment of the balance of power and the Party's priorities in Japan, as well as the effects of demands made on the Japanese Communists by China and the Soviet Union.

The Early Postwar Years, 1945-50

Contrary to what one might expect of a Communist Party with a long tradition, of enforced illegal, underground activity under a repressive police system, the Japanese Communist Party has rarely indulged in actual—as contrasted with verbal—violence. Violence in Japan has on the whole rather been the preferred strategy of right-wing extremists.

In the immediate postwar period, the Japanese Communists sought to erase the Party's prewar image of a closed, secretive, foreign-directed, radical organization. Their strategy aimed, as its principal proponent Nosaka Sanzō (the current Party Chairman) put it, at making the Party "lovable" and bringing it close to the people. This formula was appropriate in an era when the U.S. Occupation regime was making every effort to give Japan political democracy and when the Japanese Communists' legal right to work openly for their objectives was firmly guaranteed. Nosaka's strategy sought to build a united front with other non-conservative parties by playing down ideological and programmatic differences between them. It focused on Japanese rather than U.S. "imperialism" as the main enemy and viewed the struggle for power in Japan as being still in its first stage, the bourgeois-democratic revolution, which could be supported by all segments of the Japanese population except "monopoly capitalists." The Party's strategic formula thus allowed for maximum opportunities to integrate the Communist Party into the then tolerant and liberalizing Japanese political environment.

In proposing this strategy for the Party's political struggle, Nosaka took a leaf from Chinese Communist experience (he had spent most of the war years in Yenan with Mao Tse-tung and returned to Japan only in early 1946): he stressed patriotism and democratic nationalism, advocated a broad united front including the "progressive" bourgeoisie, and spoke of peaceful revolution. The results of this strategy confirmed its effectiveness. The JCP acquired a new image, which translated into increased popular support. By 1949, the Party had 100,000 members and was polling close to three million votes, about 10 percent of the total cast.

The Years of Direct, Violent Action, 1950-55

In January 1950 a new strategy of militancy and outright violence was suddenly forced upon the JCP from the outside when the Cominform journal, speaking for the Soviet and Chinese Communist parties, denounced the Japanese Party for its "grave errors." By then the international situation and conditions in Japan had undergone major changes, imposing new requirements on Communist strategy: the U.S.-Soviet alliance had given way to a cold war; in China the Communists had come to power; and in Korea an East-West military confrontation was getting under way. Like Communist parties elsewhere, the JCP was expected by Moscow and Peking to do its share to obstruct the U.S. war effort, particularly as it required the use of bases in Japan. The Japanese Communist Party was, however, the last of the Asian parties to adopt the revolutionary strategy that the CPSU and the CCP demanded of their allies abroad.

The abrupt shift in Japanese Communist strategy brought about by the open intervention of the two major Communist powers caused serious confusion within the Japanese Party. Chief strategist Nosaka and Secretary General Tokuda Kyūichi were able to ride out the storm by admitting their guilt and promising to make amends. The Cominform-recommended strategy of violent action was quickly adopted and implemented in 1950; its application reached a high point in the following two years.

Although from its inception the strategy proved a conspicuous failure, the Party was allowed to lay it aside only in 1955. During the intervening years, the JCP submitted to direct guidance from Moscow and increasingly from Peking. Alienated from its many moderate sympathizers, the Party was caught up in bitter factional strife over what tactics to employ in applying Mao's revolutionary formula in Japan. Meanwhile, the Party apparatus had moved underground; most of the top leaders sought refuge in China to escape police persecution; and a Central Directorate took over the few remaining legal Party activities. An attempt was actually made to organize a guerrilla force in Japan and to train its members in clandestine practices and subversive action (sabotage, attacks against police boxes with Molotov cocktails, and the like), to engage in terrorism, and to build—on the Chinese pattern—guerrilla bases in remote areas of Japan. The study of Mao's writings on guerrilla warfare became obligatory for all Party members.

The theoretical basis for Party strategy during those years was provided by the 1951 Thesis, a document conceived and written in Peking. It prescribed the creation of a "national liberation democratic movement" (under the slogan "Peace and Independence") against the principal enemy, which was no longer Japanese "monopoly capitalism" but "American imperialism," and urged direct action against the U.S. military presence in Japan. No longer was there any mention of peaceful revolution; instead Party members were told to struggle—violently—for peace.

This Chinese-inspired formula proved ill-suited to Japanese conditions. The Japanese government, having recovered full national sovereignty in 1952 from the Allied Occupation, had no trouble riding out the feeble Communist assault. Meanwhile, Party membership continued to drop, and electoral support dwindled as the JCP, no longer "beloved by the people," found itself persecuted and ostracized. As early as 1953, these failures prompted the JCP leaders to reexamine their policy, but it was only two years later that the Party officially abandoned the ineffective strategy of sabotage and violent revolution.

Aside from this brief episode in the Party's postwar history, the JCP has only occasionally engaged in violence, and then only in mass movements that got out of hand. Nor have the Communists recently been tempted to challenge the power of the state by calling a general strike. The Party made such an attempt only once, in the heady post-surrender atmosphere of 1947, but quickly cancelled it when confronted with the U.S. Occupation regime's determination not to let democratic freedoms degenerate into disorder.

Current Strategy

By 1955 the failure of Communist revolutionary violence in Japan had apparently become clear to the Soviet and Chinese leaders. In any case, by then this strategic formula no longer fitted their policies. Stalin (as well as the JCP's strongman, Tokuda) had died. The Chinese Communists were displaying the Bandung spirit, and Khrushchev had consolidated his power and removed Stalin from his pedestal. The JCP was thus allowed to use reason and to rethink its problems.

While the Japanese Communists abandoned the strategy of compulsory violence imposed from abroad as soon as international conditions permitted, they found it difficult to reach agreement on the answer to the three basic questions affecting Communist strategy in Japan: (1) Who should be considered the principal enemy, Japanese capitalism or U.S. "imperialism"? (2) What stage of economic development has Japanese society attained and what type of revolution should the Party therefore promote? (3) What tactics should be employed? Agreement on the answers was long in coming, only partly because a minority within the Party refused to abandon the direct approach to revolution. The major cause of the factional strife which continued to plague the JCP for many years lay in the international environment, to which the JCP continued to be highly sensitive. The late 1950's were, of course, the years of a developing Sino-Soviet rift as well as of intensive discussion among Communists everywhere regarding the meaning and role of "revisionism." This was the time when the Italian Communist leader Togliatti's structural reform theories entered Japan and found many converts among Communists and Socialists alike.

Opinion within the Japanese Party tended to polarize around two basic positions—a leftist strategy closely akin to the Chinese Communist formula and a revisionist strategy that owed much of its inspiration to the structural reform theories and was ideologically rather close to Soviet views. Thus one faction saw the principal enemy in "U.S. imperialism" while the other contended that Japan had completely regained its national independence and the fight therefore should concentrate on Japanese capitalism at home. In line with these differing analyses, one faction saw Japan in need of a "democratic revolution for national liberation" (a formula inspired by the Chinese model). The opponents viewed Japan as a fully developed, highly capitalistic country, ready for an immediate socialist revolution. The question thus became whether the Party should press for an immediate establishment of a socialist regime—an issue which even during prewar times occasioned much controversy among Japanese Marxist theorists.* Finally, regarding the tactics to be employed, one side wished to keep open the option of violent action. The other advocated exclusive use of peaceful revolutionary tactics to lead smoothly from the capitalist present to a socialist future through the gradual transformation of the power structure by a steady accumulation of minor successes achieved by an alliance of "progressive forces."

By mid-1961, the JCP had come down on the side of Marxist orthodoxy. The supporters of the structural reform theory had been expelled, some of them to join the ranks of the Socialist Party. When the Eighth Party Congress met that year, it endorsed a new program which hewed close to the views of the faction whose position accorded with the Chinese Communist view rather than with that of Western European parties. This basic policy document admitted that Japan was indeed a highly developed capitalist society, but took the position that in its dependence on the United States it was a "semi-colony" (of the United States).† This identified the principal target of Communist action as "U.S. imperialism." The Party was to work toward a people's democratic revolution of an anti-imperialist, anti-monopoly nature. The revolution was to proceed in two (uninterrupted) stages, initiated by the formation of a democratic united front composed of all but the monopoly capitalist classes and led by the JCP.

*Whether revolution in Japan should be a one-stage or a two-stage task was the subject of considerable controversy in prewar Japan. Prior to the 1932 Thesis, Japan had been viewed by the Communists as a mature capitalist society calling therefore for a one-stage, proletarian revolution. The 1932 Thesis, which set the pattern for Communist thinking in postwar Japan, defined the country as a highly developed capitalist state with substantial feudal remnants, thus requiring "a bourgeois-democratic revolution tending to develop rapidly into a socialist revolution."

†The resolution adopted on July 6, 1970 by the Eleventh Party Congress reconfirms this view of the U.S.-Japanese relationship in these terms: "Despite the rapid advance of the revival of [Japanese] militarism and imperialism, Japan has even now not regained full independence. Under the San Francisco [Peace Treaty] system, it continues to be a semi-occupied, semi-independent country chained to the U.S. imperialist policy of war and aggression. It is, as the Party Program puts it, a country which is in fact dependent on and semi-occupied by U.S. imperialism." (From *Gekkan Gakushū,* August 1970, pp. 87-88.)

As for the prescribed tactics, while it was decreed that the Party should make full use of the existing parliamentary system and opportunities, it should not feel bound to limit itself to these: the choice of violent or peaceful methods was to depend on prevailing need and circumstances. Finally and logically, the JCP was to forge a united front with other "progressive elements" under the broad and popular slogan "Peace and National Independence." What could be accomplished by such a strategy, it was argued, had been demonstrated the previous year, when Japan's largest postwar mass movement united against the U.S.-Japanese security pact and the American alliance, shook the foundations of the Kishi government, brought millions of hitherto non-politicized Japanese into the streets, and created what looked to some like a revolutionary situation. (It was overlooked that the leading force in this movement had not been the JCP but the Socialists and their labor unions, that the movement was aided by an unusual set of circumstances, and that in its aftermath the "progressive elements" failed to hold their apparent gains and subsequently suffered setbacks at the polls.)

In line with this new and generally nonviolent strategy, the JCP has ever since sought to develop the "peace and national independence" theme by directing Communist propaganda and organization against the principal "enemy," the United States. Specific propaganda themes have included:

The presence of U.S. forces in Japan and Okinawa (side effects of U.S. bases; alleged risks of retaliation from abroad including Soviet nuclear threats, etc.)

The alleged danger of nuclear war and accidents as a result of the Okinawa bases and the entry of nuclear-propelled (but described as "nuclear") U.S. warships into Japanese ports

The risks of involvement in war as a result of Japan's alliance with a power (the United States) fighting in Asia

The danger of Japan's becoming isolated, due to the U.S. alliance, in an Asia that is predominantly neutralist or Communist

The increase of tension because the Japanese permit U.S. "aggressive" bases on Japanese soil and the resulting obstacle to Sino-Japanese friendship, an essential element of stability in Asia

The alleged militarization and nuclearization of Japan through U.S.sponsored rearmament, which violates the Peace Constitution

The U.S. strengthening of a conservative, "reactionary" regime leading Japan back to a repressive police state

The "colonization" and exploitation of the Japanese people by U.S. monopoly capital and its Japanese allies

These Communist propaganda themes command some popularity, since they reflect not only the Japanese people's fears of involvement in war but permit exploitation of rising nationalism.

Communist stress on nationalist sentiments has been increasingly conspicuous in JCP strategy. It has been all the more effective since after 1966 the JCP clearly established an identity independent of both Moscow and Peking. This new image of the Communist Party as a genuinely Japanese organization having only the interest of the Japanese people at heart has become more convincing as the Party has been attentive to popular grievances—especially when such grievances could be linked to the anti-American theme.

The effort to appear more responsive to the aspirations of the ordinary citizen and to broaden the JCP's base of popular support is reflected in all aspects of Party activity. The JCP maintains consulting facilities to advise and help the citizen in daily living; in 1969, special sections were set up in the Central Committee to deal with the problems of medium and small enterprises and a department was established to concentrate on the uses of science and technology; *Akahata*, the Party daily, has been transformed from an austere, ideologically oriented organ into a newspaper dealing with a broad range of topics and providing varied fare, including a column on Japanese chess and interviews with entertainers. Gradually the memory of the Party's years of extremism is thus being superseded by the image of what Nosaka once had called the "lovable Party."

Since the Party's direct political influence is still small, it is eager to enter into an alliance with the Japanese Socialist Party (JSP), which commands the largest popular support among the opposition forces. At first glance, the chances of Socialist-Communist cooperation would seem excellent, for both parties profess faith in Marxism, both are opposed to Japan's current foreign policies, particularly to Japan's American alliance, and both are violently opposed to the present conservative regime. But for a number of reasons cooperation has proven difficult to establish on anything but a temporary or specific-issue basis.

In the first place, the Socialists have been less in need of Communist assistance than vice versa. They also recognize the dangers of cooperation with the Communists. They remember bitter experiences in the past; and the Communists, even when operating in alliance with the Socialists, do not cease proselytizing among Socialist supporters by criticizing the Socialist leadership as "revisionist" or "petty bourgeois." At the same time, any close association between the two Marxist parties risks splitting the Socialists, as in fact it has done in the past, for the JSP is really two parties: its left wing acts more militantly and is more Peking-oriented than the Communists, while its right wing abhors any dealings with the Communists. The Socialist leadership is well aware that the uneasy alliance between the two wings of the JSP (which are engaged in a continuous struggle for party control) can easily be strained or broken by any agreement to work permanently or closely with the Communists.

Communist efforts to build a permanent alliance through a united front from above continue, of course, but meanwhile the Communists place heavy emphasis on work from below—"prompting from above and united action from below," as the JCP puts it. This principle has been successfully applied in specific anti-U.S. campaigns (such as the 1969 joint anti-U.S. effort on the Okinawa issue), as well as in national and local elections.

The Japanese Communists have made full use of the forum provided by nationally and locally elected bodies in which the Party is represented. They use these bodies as sounding boards for their anti-American themes, taking up such concrete issues as the population's dissatisfaction with land requisitions for U.S. bases, the disturbing jet noise of U.S. planes, the entry of U.S. nuclear-propelled warships, aircraft accidents, U.S. control over Okinawa, and the like, but they also vent the grievances of the electorate in other matters—especially when these can somehow be linked to the anti-U.S. theme.

Communist parliamentary effort is always accompanied by a propaganda campaign outside the Diet, as reflected in such activities as the frequent distribution of Party pamphlets. Some of the titles issued in the short period between mid-December 1967 and the end of January

1968 give an idea of the range of this continuing program: "Ten Questions and Answers About the JCP's Position on National Independence," "Corruption and Graft in the Satō Cabinet," "The War of Aggression in Vietnam and Japan," "The JCP's Program for Improving Living Conditions," "Ten Questions and Answers About the Workers and Politics," "Ten Questions and Answers About the Farmer and the JCP," "How to Bring Happiness to Women and Children," "Strength and Hope for Working Women," "Mother Let Us All Persevere—Words for the Working Farm Woman," "How to Protect Livelihood and Eliminate Sickness," "For the Advance of the Struggle of Workers in Small and Medium Business."

Communist activity in the legislative bodies also is always backed by thorough study and investigation of the potentially controversial issues. A special Communist Diet member Committee carefully prepares interpellations drawing systematically on research done by the various subsections of the Central Committee. Communist interventions in the Diet therefore are often effective in exposing sensitive aspects of government policy, particularly as it relates to the alliance with the United States. In recent years, Party representatives in the Diet (among them the experienced parliamentarian Chairman Nosaka) have sought to appear not merely as critics of the established order but as representatives of a party dedicated to constructive contributions to the legislative process. A report in *Akahata* on May 15, 1968, for example, listed the Communist representatives' position (compared with the positions of other parties) on major pieces of legislation during the 58th Diet session (early 1968). The tabulation indicated that the JCP approved 25.5 percent of the bills examined, opposed 64.0 percent, and abstained on 10.5 percent. (The corresponding figures for the other opposition parties were as follows: JSP 68.0 percent, 32.0 percent, and 0; Kōmeitō, 72.4 percent, 27.6 percent, and 0; DSP 76.6 percent, 23.4 percent, and 0—demonstrating the high degree of consensus politics being practiced in Japan.)

As long as Communist strength in the Diet remains below the legal requirement for securing representation in all Diet working committees, the JCP is excluded from some of the politically more profitable areas of parliamentary activity. However, even in its present position, it derives numerous advantages from participation in the parliamentary process. Not the least of these is its ability to serve as a channel of propaganda and a sounding board for the anti-American policies of its many auxiliary organizations, such as the Afro-Asian Solidarity Committee and the Japan Council Against A and H Bombs, and to make their voices heard in the general press and other mass media, which are anyway inclined to play up views critical of the government.

The JCP, as a party out of power, has rarely faced the dilemma of whether to give priority to the national interest or to long-range and worldwide Communist objectives in considering issues confronting Japan. One of the few exceptions has been the unresolved territorial issue between the Soviet Union and Japan. At first—and true to its tradition—the JCP took the Soviet side at the expense of Japan's national interest, but it did so in a way that so obscured the issue that it did not have to pay too heavy a political price. More recently, in line with its independent stance, the Party has not hesitated to criticize the Soviet Union. Since its estrangement from both Moscow and Peking, the JCP acts as a party whose primary responsibility is to the Japanese people rather than to its foreign comrades. This attitude is beginning to bring good political returns.

Peripheral Organizations

The organizational apparatus of the JCP has been described and evaluated in Chapter Two. The Party's inner core is surrounded by a multiplicity of organizations in which Communist influence ranges from controlling to substantial, either from the numerical weight of members under Party control or because their superior organizational skills and centralized direction give them influence well beyond their numbers. [1]

Occupational Organizations. Japan's trade-union movement has long been split into two major organizations: an anti-Communist federation of unions, allied to the Democratic Socialist Party (DSP), particularly strong in private enterprise; and the larger Sōhyō federation, which is directed mostly by individuals close to the Japanese Socialist Party (JSP). The Communists have never been able to capture more than about one-fourth of the vast Sōhyō organization, and their present control or influence probably extends to no more than a fifth of the total. However, even under its predominantly Socialist direction, Sōhyō is a valuable asset to the JCP. In the first place, it is sufficiently radical, politicized, and Marxist-oriented to permit cooperation with the Communists on issues related to the "struggle against American imperialism and Japanese monopoly capital." Second, a number of important member unions are so heavily infiltrated by Communists that their influence must be taken into account whenever the Sōhyō leaders formulate policies.

The Communist-influenced unions are concentrated in certain branches of industry, particularly among workers in government agencies and services as well as in public corporations sponsored by the government. Communist influence is powerful among government workers in tax services, in the construction industry, in telecommunications, and in the Justice, Labor, and Transportation ministries. In unions in these employment sectors Party membership reportedly ranged from 10 to 25 percent in 1968. Less important but still significant was JCP influence in the following government workers' unions: Agriculture Ministry Workers Union, Japan Teachers Union (total membership 588,000, of whom about 10,000 were Party members), Government Railroad Workers Union (7,000 Party members), National Telecommunications Workers Union (4,000 Party members), and National Electrical and Communications Workers Union (about 4,000 Party members).

In private enterprise the following important fields of union activity were reported to have heavy Communist influence, since their executive bodies were for the most part dominated by JCP members: paper industry, automobile industry, metal industry, printing, broadcasting and television, and casual labor. Substantial numbers of Party members are also found in the following unions: Japan Newspaper Unions Federation (one-third of whose officers in 1968 were reportedly Party members), Japan Coal Mine Workers Union, Japan Private Railroad Workers Union, Japan Dock Workers Union, and Synthetic Chemical Industry Workers Union.

Communist influence among organized farm laborers is substantially less. Thanks to the Occupation-sponsored land reform and the government's price support policies, most Japanese farmers are prosperous and own their land. There is little reason for them to participate in militant union activity. Whatever grievances they may have are neither acute nor easily politically exploitable. The major exceptions are cases where agricultural land is being requisitioned by U.S. or Japanese military forces, particularly on the fringes of the big cities where labor unions can be called in to support and give organizational backbone to protest movements. It is estimated that about 10 percent of the predominantly youthful membership of the small (20,000 members) Agricultural Workers Union Federation belonged to the JCP in late 1966; that organization was listed in official Japanese reports as being under Communist influence. The more important Japan Farmers Union Federation

(250,000 members) was reported to have only "indirect Communist influence."

Communist success in dominating groups and organizations representing the interest of the intellectuals and the professions has been marked. University students especially have long been useful to the JCP as a reservoir for Party recruitment and as a group that can be easily mobilized for protest movements and mass demonstrations. Highly intellectualized and idealistic, Japanese students tend to be attracted to "perfect" and "universal" formulas for building a good society; Marxist-Leninist influence is pronounced among them. The Zengakuren federation of student self-government organizations has long been the largest and politically most militant student movement.[2] It has also been distinguished by its fiery devotion to ultra-radical interpretations of Marxist philosophy. The organization's weakness—from the JCP point of view—is its tendency to break up into feuding factions, each more extremist than the other and highly critical of the Communist Party itself as being bureaucratic, compromising, and part of the Establishment. The JCP thus continuously asserts and reasserts its control in this sphere without ever gaining total or lasting success, but even the Zengakuren's Communist factions violently opposed to the JCP are useful to the Party in their dedication to reckless actions. Against the backdrop of Maoist campus rampages, the student groups under the control of the Party's Democratic Youth League appear to the public the very models of moderation, thus improving the Party's popular image and increasing its influence.

Currently the Zengakuren is split four ways, into the Yoyogi faction (named after the site of the JCP's Tokyo headquarters) and the three major (in turn internally split) rival anti-Yoyogi groups. It is estimated that the JCP-oriented faction controls about 65 percent of the total of about 500 student self-government associations. This percentage represents between a quarter million and a half million students—a sizable reservoir for militant mass action, although only some 10,000-15,000 of these students actually belong to the Party's youth organization.

Communist influence is also pronounced in many organizations representing non-student intellectuals, trained professional workers, or workers associated with the professions. In Japan the outlook of these groups tends to be far to the left of that of the ordinary citizen. They are generally believers in Marxism and are sympathetic to the causes for which the JCP agitates under the motto "Peace, Democracy, and Independence." Thus Communist influence is exceptionally strong among

Japanese scientists, journalists, writers, and artists, and somewhat less so among doctors and lawyers. The principal organizations in this category include the following (membership shown in parentheses): Democratic Medical Workers Federation (7,500 members, of whom 2,200 were reportedly Party members as of late 1966), Japan Scientists Council (5,000 members), Japan Democratic Literature League (2,300), New Japan Doctors Association (700), Japan Medical Workers Union Conference (65,000), Free Lawyers Guild (350), Young Jurists' Association (perhaps 2,000 members), National Musical Workers Federation Liaison Conference (membership not known), National Workers Motion Picture Conference (80,000), National Performing Workers Liaison Conference (100,000), and Japan Journalists League (1,500).

Special Groups. The JCP has long made concentrated and fairly successful efforts to mobilize women and youth for its purposes. In late 1968, the Party controlled the New Japan Women's Society of 90,000 members, of whom one-fifth were estimated to be Party members. Its direct influence in the much larger (250,000 members) Federation of Japan Women's Organizations and in some smaller, specialized women's groups such as the Women's Democratic Clubs (2,000 members) was also significant, since JCP members occupied a majority of these organizations' key positions. While the total membership of such organizations cannot compare with that of the trade unions, it provides an adequate base for Communist campaigns of special interest to women, such as peace and anti-nuclear demonstrations or protest movements against the rise in the cost of living.

The Party pays special attention to youth, as is shown by the previously discussed successful membership drive among teenagers and young adults. Its youth association in late 1969 numbered more than 200,000 members, of whom 60,000 were estimated to be Party members, making it the largest politically oriented youth organization in Japan. The Party's heavy infiltration among the college-student population has already been mentioned; it has also begun to sink roots among the upperclassmen of Japan's high schools. The number of Communists in high schools reportedly exceeded 10,000 in 1969. In addition, the Party has sought to influence working youth by organizing special training and lecture courses (Marxism-Leninism, foreign languages, etc.) and arranging special entertainment (concerts, chorus groups, folk dancing, travel, motion pictures) and reading circles such as the Young People's Reading Clubs (37,000 members).

Traditionally, the JCP has worked among the two substantial minority groups suffering from discrimination, the former outcasts and the Korean residents. In the case of the former, however, the Party's success has been consistently eclipsed by that of the Socialists. An extension of the prewar Communist-influenced organization devoted to the defense of outcasts' rights continues to be active, but reliable figures regarding its strength are unavailable because of the Japanese sensitivity to this particular issue. The JCP has been particularly active among this group in Western Japan (Kyoto, Osaka, and Okayama) where members are most numerous. This factor may in part account for Communist electoral successes in these districts.

The JCP has been more successful among the Korean community in Japan, most of whose 600,000 members are of working-class origin and fill the less desirable occupations. Most severely hit by economic crises because of lack of job security, they have a high unemployment rate' even in ordinary times. As a result, a majority of the Korean residents (organized in the General Federation of Korean Residents in Japan) are in sympathy with the North Korean Communist regime and work closely with the JCP, strengthened in this bond by their prewar association.

Organizations Devoted to Specific Issues. To reaffirm its traditional ties to the Communist movement abroad, the JCP has actively promoted international friendship societies directed particularly toward the Soviet Union and Communist China. In 1966, i.e., before the Communist front organizations split into pro-JCP and pro-Maoist wings, the Japan-Communist China Friendship Association counted 36,000 members; the Japan-Soviet Association about half that number; and the Japan-North Korea Association roughly 9,000 members. These associations have served the JCP in a number of ways. They have provided facilities for contacts with sympathizers and potential Party members. They have also offered a meeting ground with influential conservative businessmen interested in expanding commercial exchanges with the Communist countries. (In the case of trade with Communist China and the Soviet Union, the friendship associations have been supplemented by special trade-promotion organizations, which reportedly also served as channels for funds to JCP coffers until relations with Moscow and Peking soured.) Further, these associations have provided the Party with prestige (important non-Communists, including an ex-prime minister, have participated in them), and with means of exerting pressure on the Japanese government to move toward normalization of diplomatic relations with the Communist countries. The Sino-Soviet split has recently inserted a strong wedge into the relatively harmonious working relationship of Communists and Socialists within the friendship associations. As a result, each of the major associations has split into at least two rival organizations along the lines of their positions in the Sino-Soviet conflict.

Similar splits have occurred in the several organizations which the JCP has created or sponsored to propagate the "peace" theme. They include the Japan Peace Committee (with 37,000 members, of whom about one-third were Party members in late 1966), the League for the Protection of the [Peace] Constitution, and, most important, Gensuikyō, the Japan Council Against A and H Bombs, which was established as a nonpartisan organization in the wake of the U.S. nuclear testing at Bikini. The Gensuikyō is a federation of many groups (including prominently many labor unions) which, on paper at least, represented in late 1966 close to a million persons opposed to nuclear testing and similar armament. Gensuikyō has been an effective means of keeping the Japanese people's "nuclear allergy" sensitive and an important pressure group opposing any attempt to rearm Japan with advanced weapons systems, particularly with nuclear arms. Beyond this, Communist influence has made the organization an instrument for a whole range of anti-American propaganda and activity and has provided a rallying point for anti-American elements. But this Communist auxiliary too has fallen victim to conflicts among members of Japan's left over the Sino-Soviet controversy. It has been reduced to a politically less effective— since purely JCP-controlled—organization from which not only genuine nonpolitical pacifists but also the Socialists have withdrawn. Currently, two other organizations vie with Gensuikyō in leading the movement against nuclear armament and for worldwide abolition of nuclear weapons. Each is so strongly politicized and identified with a particular foreign policy position that formation of a united front on the nuclear issue has become increasingly difficult.

The Ideological Climate

Communist and Communist-influenced organizations in Japan operate under a set of favorable ideological conditions. For historical reasons and despite Japan's rapid economic growth and physical modernization, Marxism remains the single most potent intellectual and political belief system in postwar Japan. Its influence is pronounced in certain key areas of society, including the universities, the mass media, and generally the intellectual professions, as well as among organized labor. Operating in a social system in which leadership tends to be recruited through a master-disciple or leader-henchman relationship, Marxist influence in the universities tends to be self-perpetuating, though it is gradually waning even among Japanese academics as Japan loses its insular status and as the realities of modern life tend to contradict Marxist doctrine and predictions.

The Party thus shares certain common beliefs and assumptions regarding the evolution of society with a large and influential portion of the population outside its ranks, and thus it finds an environment that facilitates Communist indoctrination and propaganda. Conditions may also favor the Party's effort to build a united front with other opponents of the established political and capitalist economic order. A brief examination of these potential allies and the JCP's successes to date in forging a united front, however, reveals the very real obstacles to integration of the Communists into a broad popular front.

The JCP's Competitors. The results of the recent (December 27, 1969) national elections to the House of Representatives provide the best barometer of current popular support for the JCP and its political rivals.

In the aggregate, the total vote of the opposition parties (i.e., all but the LDP and the conservative independents) has fluctuated between about one-half and one-third of the vote cast, although because of the electoral system this has resulted in a much smaller number of seats in the Diet than a strictly proportionate distribution would produce. The JSP is by far the most important opposition party and has been so throughout the postwar period, but in recent years its vote percentage has declined, confirming the prediction that Japan would evolve into a multi-party system.

TABLE 4. *1969 House of Representatives Election*
(486 seats contested)

Party	Vote (millions)	% of Total vote	Seats Won
Liberal Democratic Party (LDP)	22.38	47.63	288
Japan Socialist Party (JSP)	10.07	21.44	90
Kōmeitō	5.12	10.91	47
Democratic Socialist Party (DSP)	3.64	7.74	31
Japan Communist Party (JCP)	3.20	6.81	14
Independents (mostly conservatives who subsequently joined the LDP fraction)	2.49	5.30	16

The JSP, as the opposition force par excellence, would appear to be the natural ally of the JCP for other reasons. It also believes in a division of the world into the forces of socialism—equated with "peace"—and the forces of capitalism—equated with "war"; consequently, it is also strongly opposed to Japan's U.S. alliance and to the presence of U.S. forces on Japanese soil. Moreover the JSP, like the JCP, opposes Japanese rearmament, advocates a neutralist policy for Japan, and urges recognition of Communist China and generally closer relations with the Communist countries. Considering its strong position in the ranks of labor and among Japan's intellectuals and its substantial support from small business, the JSP is obviously the essential factor in the success or failure of a united front in Japan. However, as explained earlier, the Socialists have consistently refused to enter into a permanent alliance with the Communists. At best the JCP has only been able to obtain a series of temporary, case-by-case working arrangements with its Marxist competitor on such issues as the return of Okinawa to Japanese control, action against basing B-52's in Japan, opposition to nuclear armament, and campaigns against the Vietnam war and against an extension of the security pact with the United States.

Such joint actions have often been effective, as evidenced in the 1960 mass demonstrations against the security pact and its sponsor, the Kishi government. Socialist-Communist cooperation has also produced results in electoral campaigns. For example, both Tokyo and Kyoto currently have "progressive" governors, largely thanks to a JCP-JSP electoral alliance. The JCP, while seeking to make joint actions a point of departure for closer cooperation in all spheres, is nevertheless reluctant to drop its campaigns in left-wing organizations and in the Socialist ranks against the JSP's policies and leadership. Issues on which the Communists and Socialists currently disagree and which the JCP is using in criticism of its potential ally, include the principal target of the political struggle (the JSP identifies it as Japanese rather than U.S. capitalism), the role of the nuclear test ban (the JCP endorsed it, the JCP did not), and the proper evaluation of the Chinese Great Cultural Revolution (which the radical Socialists view with much admiration and sympathy).

That the basic outlook of the two parties is similar can be seen in the vacillation of many voters between support of the JSP and the JCP. This was strikingly illustrated in the 1949 national elections, when a substantial portion of disgruntled Socialist supporters switched over to the Communists, only to return a few years later to the Socialist fold. A similar phenomenon is probably behind the JCP's success in the December 1969 elections, although it is conceivable that that election constituted a turning point in the Socialist-Communist balance of forces. The well-organized, well-funded JCP is beginning to assume the former JSP role of champion of the working class. The Japanese Communists have for a number of years successfully worked at the grass-roots level, listening to local grievances and playing on the nationalist theme, while their Socialist rivals were occupied with factional struggles and seemed to have lost all sense of reality. With its new, improved image, the JCP may become more attractive to the voter than the JSP if both parties continue on their present course.

In a recent television interview (January 2, 1970), JCP Chairman Nosaka expressed his conviction that Japan would first become "an independent and peaceful country" and only after some time would establish socialism. Despite this gradualistic approach and the advocacy of a "people's democratic coalition government" in which the existing parties would work together, the Communists find it difficult to interest the other opposition parties in uniting with them in a popular front.

The second Socialist party, the Democratic Socialists (DSP), represents moderate social democratic elements who have moved in and out of the JSP orbit. In the past several years, the DSP appears to have gained in confidence and popular support, and there are indications that the Japanese voter is ready to listen more to the moderate socialist reformers and believers in peaceful evolution. The essentially middle-of-the-road DSP has frequently made common cause with its rival Socialists (although it has just as frequently given support to the conservative position), but it has adamantly refused to sit down at the same table with the Communists. It is difficult to see how the Communists could mollify such staunch anti-Communists; this may be the reason why the JCP now seems to have just about written off the Democratic Socialists as potential allies in a popular front and why they have begun to label them "pro-American" and "conservative."

A question mark on the current Japanese political scene and in Japan's future is the Kōmeitō party. At this point it is not even clear whether this recently created organization—the political arm of the nationalist Buddhist Sōkagakkai movement—should be termed "centrist," "rightist," or "left." At any rate, the efficiently run and well-financed party has grown rapidly, is an unusually dynamic and effective proselytizer, and is extremely well disciplined. It is also suspected of ambitions beyond Japan because of its ties with the Sōkagakkai parent organization, which is actively establishing chapters throughout Asia and America. The Kōmeitō draws support from many of the same groups to which the JCP seeks to appeal: those baffled by the rapid social and economic change, those who are disgusted with the graft and corruption so often associated with Japanese politics (the party's name means "Clean Government Party"), and all those who search for direction and a sense of participation in a group of like-minded men. In its social base, the Kōmeitō thus competes with the JCP in the lower economic brackets, among farmers and workers and the lower stratum of urban society (although it is also making inroads into other groups). Because of its Buddhist and nationalist origins, its missionary zeal, and its superior organization, the Kōmeitō has grown steadily in influence—despite forecasts of imminent stagnation—and has developed into a formidable rival for all Japanese political parties, including the Communists. The latter have until recently sought to bring the Kōmeitō into a united front against the government on such issues as rearmament, nuclear weapons, and normalization of diplomatic relations with China—issues on which the new party appears to agree with the JCP and the Socialists.

But the Kōmeitō has remained a political force beholden only to its own leaders and quite unwilling to submit to outside direction or advice. Increasing rivalry has caused the Communists to criticize the Kōmeitō as "potentially fascist" and "an enemy of freedom." Although the presence or absence of the Kōmeitō may well be crucial to the success of any anti-government alliance of opposition forces, the conflict between the two parties has been sharpening. Thus, during the

1969 election campaign, the JCP distributed leaflets accusing the Kō-meitō members of having turned into an anti-Communist vanguard, of "carrying the *geba-bō*" (i.e., the wooden staff used as a weapon by the student radicals) under their robes,* and of mouthing Buddhist pieties while preaching violence (in contrast the Communist Party was depict-ed as a paragon of nonviolence). No doubt, the Kōmeitō has stepped into the vacuum left by the almost total eclipse of Japan's prewar ultranationalist, messianic movements. At any rate, it may be on a collision course with the JCP.

The JCP and the Japanese Government

Ever since the dismal failure of its direct, violent challenge to the estab-lished order more than a decade ago, the JCP has become increasingly realistic in its appraisal of conditions in Japan although not abandoning its Marxist-Leninist convictions. The Party is no longer in doubt about the strength of the government's position and the effectiveness of the state apparatus, which, despite some infiltration, has remained essential-ly impregnable to Communist subversion. The Communists continue to challenge the government whenever possible and preferably in alliance with other opposition parties, applying constant pressure to sensitive spots. Yet, they remain within the limits of the law and avoid excesses which might lose them public support and provide the government with a pretext for repressive legislation or anti-Communist action. At the same time, the Communists are patiently attempting to lay the founda-tion for future united opposition—the "united national democratic front"—which, they hope, will eventually produce an anti-government mass movement that can establish a "democratic coalition government" under Communist control.

The Party continues to adhere to its ideological positions, but it has learned that to preach Marxism-Leninism is insufficient to gain political power. While playing on popular fears of war and on such themes as "national independence" or "defense of democracy" is effective in the Japanese context, the Party leaders have come to realize that more attention must be given to the bread-and-butter issues that determine the outcome of elections. Much of the Party's effort is now directed toward a realistic assessment of national conditions and the formulation of appropriate programs. No longer does the Party merely oppose the

*Quoted from official JCP campaign handbill in the possession of the author.

government on all issues and legislation but now confronts it with its own bills. For example, the JCP recently announced a Communist social security bill, and has issued its own program to solve the ever more serious urban ills which plague Japan as a result of the tremendous growth of the cities.

While the Socialists flounder hopelessly in theoretical discussions and utterly unrealistic policy positions, the Japanese Communists, who once also operated in a world of insulating illusions, have made serious efforts to correct this weakness. This can be illustrated by a comparison of the two parties' treatment of the issue of Japan's national security; this has been a focal point of public discussion ever since the anti-security pact riots of 1960 and especially after June 1970 when it became known that the renewed U.S.-Japan security pact may be reviewed annually by either of the contracting parties.

Both opposition parties eventually hope to bring down the government over the issue of the future of the American alliance and have been preparing for this on organizational, political, and propaganda levels. Meanwhile, the Japanese government has sought to place the issue squarely before the people, pointing out that the security pact with the United States is a necessity for militarily weak Japan, kept so by the opposition forces' refusal to allow a stronger defense establishment. The Socialists counter these arguments with their highly idealistic answer that all Japan needs to insure its security is to abolish its Self Defense Forces and follow a policy of absolute unarmed neutrality. The Communists, on the other hand, have issued a national security program of their own that does not deny the need to protect Japan's independence by maintaining military forces. Rather, they argue, the present Self Defense Forces operating under the U.S.-Japan security pact merely invite attack or risk being turned into instruments of imperialist aggression. The JCP insists, therefore, that the pact must be terminated, that relations with the Socialist countries must be normalized, but that Japan must maintain a military force in order to protect its national independence against "imperialist aggression." The Party has gone one step farther in explaining to the Japanese people what it has in store for them: recently it drafted a constitution for a "People's Republic of Japan."

Changes in tactics, however, should not obscure the fact that the JCP remains a prisoner of its Marxist-Leninist convictions. Ideological obstacles to full adaptation of the Party's philosophy to Japanese conditions are reinforced by the JCP's traditional devotion to the cause of "international communism," although an increasing number of Communists in Japan are beginning to doubt whether this concept retains any validity in a world of conflicting Chinese and Soviet interpretations of the "universal truth" and amidst the clash of diverging Communist national interests.

In the past, the JCP has distinguished itself by its slavish devotion to the defense of Soviet interests and policy positions. Only the model and the mentor changed when the Party in the 1950's turned from Moscow to Peking. Until quite recently, therefore, the JCP had always acted with one eye on the reactions of its foreign Communist sponsors, sacrificing if necessary its own interests. Thus, after 1950, the Party took a virtual death plunge into violent action against the government and U.S. forces because Moscow and Peking demanded such action. Or, to point to a more recent example, the Japanese Communists (then following Peking's rather than Moscow's instructions) opposed the partial nuclear test ban at great damage to their Party and in complete disregard of Japanese national sentiment.

That the JCP has been receptive to the demands of foreign Communist parties will be more fully examined in Chapter Five. Yet it would be inaccurate to assert that as a result the Party has been following policies which otherwise it would never have adopted. Given Marxist-Leninist premises and the ideological basis on which the JCP has been operating all these years, the principal foreign Communist demand—struggle against U.S. "imperialism and all its manifestations"—would have been endorsed anyway by the Japanese Party. Thus, the Communists' attempts to hamper the U.S. war effort in Vietnam and to engage in anti-war propaganda among U.S. servicemen in Japan flow as much from the Party's convictions as from the demands of Communist forces outside Japan.

One might say that the Party's policies have been somewhat vitiated by an overemphasis on issues that are of particular interest to foreign Communist powers. Only quite recently—since about 1966 or 1967—has the JCP leadership begun to think more independently of foreign Communist advice. This has come to be reflected in a lessened responsiveness to demands from abroad, in greater emphasis on the requirements of the political struggle at home, and generally in an intensification of the national theme. The conflicting pressures of Moscow and Peking have confronted the JCP with the need for a re-examination of its past policies and priorities. The Party leadership appears to have emerged from this with the desire to build a Communist party that seeks truly to become a part of the Japanese scene by focusing more attention on the problems at home.

5: JCP Conflict and Integration with the International Environment

The Communist parties which have most consistently and strongly influenced JCP leaders and their policies are those of the Soviet Union and Communist China. The sharp conflict between those two parties during the last decade has caused the JCP to reexamine its traditional subservience to communism outside Japan. And by forcing the JCP to choose sides, the Sino-Soviet rift has hastened the Party's evolution toward autonomy.

This evolution has proceeded through six stages: (1) from post-surrender reconstitution of the Party in the fall of 1945 to the end of 1949, a period of minimal foreign Communist interference; (2) between 1950 and the middle of the decade, when JCP strategy was completely under foreign direction and Peking, with Moscow's consent, appears to have been in actual charge of the Japanese Party; (3) from the late 1950's to late 1961, when the JCP sought to maintain neutrality between its Soviet and Chinese sponsors; (4) from early 1962 to early 1963, when the Japanese Communists leaned increasingly toward Peking and began to criticize Khrushchev's ideological and policy positions; (5) the era of the JCP's substantial identification with the Chinese Communists from 1963 well into 1965; and (6) what may well prove to be the age of autonomy, beginning from about December 1965, when the JCP for the first time openly criticized both Moscow and Peking. Not all the details of the triangular relationship are known outside higher Party circles, but the number of defections from Party ranks during the past decade or two allow insights into those events. Moreover the JCP, Moscow, and Peking all have publicly engaged in polemics and issued many illuminating internal party documents.

Effect on Party Leadership

In prewar times, the leaders of the Japanese Communist movement were always selected by Moscow via the Comintern. They were likewise removed from their positions whenever they proved too independent-minded or showed tendencies of becoming critical of Moscow-recommended strategy. In the process, the Japanese Communist movement lost a number of able men, developed a tradition of foreign orientation, and became alienated from its national environment.

Whether Moscow participated in the postwar reconstruction of the Party is not clear, but without exception those who assumed control of the organization had been reared in the Comintern tradition and were well known in Moscow as proven defenders of Soviet interests. They included the late Secretary General Tokuda Kyūichi, and top Party leaders Shiga Yoshio, Nosaka Sanzō (currently Party Chairman), Miya-moto Kenji (now Chairman of the Presidium) and the Moscow-educated Hakamada Satomi (Vice Chairman of the Presidium).

Thus Moscow had no reason to suspect the loyalty of the postwar Japanese Party's leaders. At first, therefore, their policies were apparently little scrutinized in Moscow, especially since the Soviet Union was then preoccupied with Europe. At any rate, Japan, under American Occupation and cut off from contacts with the outside world, was beyond Soviet reach. Moscow asserted its control openly for the first time in January 1950, when a Cominform article accused the Japanese Party of following the wrong path. This Soviet intervention[1] (soon seconded by the Chinese Communists) produced the shift in Japanese Communist strategy that was desired by Moscow and Peking. To judge by the reactions of most of the prominent Japanese Communists at the time, the Japanese leadership felt that in the face of joint Soviet-Chinese criticism of its policies it should not resist foreign Communist pressures.

In 1950 the JCP leadership behaved as it always had in the past when confronted with Soviet demands or advice. Nor did this situation basically change until the latter part of that decade, when the implications of the Sino-Soviet conflict could no longer be overlooked. As late as 1955, Nosaka spoke of "the importance and the need . . . of listening to the words of the peoples and parties of the two countries [i.e., the USSR and Communist China] ."[2] Soviet policies continued to have the unquestioned support of the JCP, although the actual direction of Japanese Communist affairs shifted more and more to Peking. At first this may have been merely the result of Soviet acquiescence in a division of labor by which the Chinese Communists would assume primary responsibility for the control of Communist movements in the Far East. However, as tensions began to build between Moscow and Peking, the

Japanese Communist leaders for the first time had to respond to the contending pulls of two rival Communist authorities. From then on, both Moscow and Peking made strenuous efforts to establish a monopoly of influence over JCP leadership. For a number of reasons, including the greater affinity the Japanese felt for the Chinese than for the Russians, Peking had the advantage in this competition until the mid-1960's. Then the JCP seemed to swing back toward Moscow as the ruthlessly dictatorial and unrealistic behavior of Mao and his aides forced a rupture of relations.

Sino-Soviet rivalry over the JCP has had a temporarily destabilizing effect on the Japanese Party's leadership. The victory of pro-Peking forces within the JCP during the early 1960's meant, of course, the elimination from leading Party posts of those men whose preferred strategy or ideological outlook was closer to Moscow than to Peking. The JCP thus lost a number of leaders and cadres, among them several Central Committee members, who had been attracted by the structural reform theories of Togliatti and by other aspects of what Peking attacked as "revisionism." In the aftermath of the 1964 international and intra-party controversy over the nuclear test ban, Shiga Yoshio, a staunch supporter of the Moscow position since the early days of the Communist movement and one of its leading figures, was expelled from the Party for his open support of the treaty. As relations between the JCP and the CPSU were severed for all practical purposes during 1964, Shiga established his own Communist group (the "Voice of Japan"). It was clearly in the Soviet camp and had Moscow's full support. Another result of the Party's growing Peking orientation was that high Party posts were opened to men who had been trained in China or had long been sponsored by the Chinese Communists. These were mostly younger men, all of whom were militant in the Peking manner. They moved into such key positions as editorship of the Party organ and direction of the Party Personnel and Finance sections.

In 1965 many experts concluded that the JCP, having evicted its pro-Soviet faction, had become a satellite of the Chinese Communists (from whom it was then receiving substantial funds). It was assumed that thenceforth the JCP would subscribe unhesitatingly to everything Peking might advocate with regard to Japanese or international Communist strategy. Developments since then have shown that such an assessment underestimated the growing strength of a trend toward independence of outside Communist influence.[3]

The majority of the Japanese Communist leaders felt (and continue to feel) a greater affinity for Peking than for Moscow, but an increasingly influential group among them has sought a position outside the two great Communist power blocs and alongside such Communist parties as those of North Korea, North Vietnam, Rumania, Cuba, and Italy. These "independents" in the JCP appear to have evolved rather gradually from an originally neutralist position between Moscow and Peking. Today they include the top leaders of the Japanese Party, including Miyamoto, Nosaka, and Hakamada in addition to other, lesser-known members. In a power struggle that resembled their struggle against the Moscow faction during 1964, these men had succeeded two years later in eliminating those under the control of Peking, among them such important figures as the late Tokuda's son-in-law, Nishizawa Ryūichi, and Anzai Kuraji, former chief of the Party's Personnel Section.

As in the case of the pro-Moscow group, the Party's Peking faction had the support of its foreign sponsor and tenaciously continued the fight even after expulsion from the Party ranks. After the spring of 1966, when negotiations broke down in Peking between then Secretary General Miyamoto and the top stratum of the Chinese hierarchy (including Mao Tse-tung and Chou En-lai), the Chinese mobilized all their assets in Japan to bring the JCP back under Peking's control. They used physical violence against the JCP's official representatives in Peking; employed dissident JCP elements residing in Peking to launch a radio campaign against the Party leaders; and gave organizational, financial, and propaganda support to an attempt of the pro-Peking faction to split the Party by establishing throughout Japan Party chapters calling themselves "left" and "true Marxist-Leninist". They vilified the independent JCP leadership as "bourgeois," "revisionist," "parliamentary cretins" conspiring with Soviet and Japanese reactionaries; they split and reorganized Communist front organizations, withheld trade from firms friendly to the JCP, and stirred up extremist leftist elements in the Zengakuren student groups against the JCP. They also threw support behind the left wing of the Japanese Socialist Party to counterbalance the JCP's influence among the extremist left and to prevent Communist-Socialist cooperation except on Peking's terms. Peking still has not abandoned its challenge to the JCP leadership. On September 18, 1968, the CCP's official daily, *Jen-min Jih-pao*, went so far as to call for the establishment of a new and "truly Marxist-Leninist organization in Japan." An organization that presumably answers the call came into being late in 1969.[4]

Soviet and Chinese attempts to reassert control over the JCP, even if ultimately failures, have had some effect. The Party has lost a number of its members (probably no more than a few thousand) and several of its more militant cadres as well as the leaders of its right and left wings. It now confronts pro-Moscow and pro-Peking splinter groups which seek to undermine its position as the leading Communist organization in Japan. On the other hand, the sloughing off of the Party's right and left wings may have increased its homogeneity and thus its ability to pursue an autonomous course, irrespective of foreign pressures. In contrast to the situation in 1950, when Party leaders immediately bowed to the reprimands of Moscow and Peking, the present leadership (much of which is the same as that of 1950—in itself indicative of the evolution of the Japanese Party) seems capable of maintaining its independent line.

Clearly the Party leadership's tone and style of operations have changed during the past several years, with heavy stress on the Party's independence. Chairman Nosaka, in his statement of July 15, 1967, on the occasion of the JCP's forty-fifth anniversary, set the tone for many subsequent Party declarations when he said:

> . . .to hold fast to this autonomous and independent stand is the absolutely indispensable prerequisite on the part of our Party. . . .Revolution in Japan is something the Japanese people ought to achieve by themselves. We must in learning from the experiences and theories of foreign revolutionary movements stand on a basis of independence and critical judgment. To apply foreign experience blindly and automatically . . . will produce endless evils. . . .[5]

For a Japanese Communist party leader—especially one like Nosaka, reared in the Comintern tradition—it is quite a departure to warn against "big-power chauvinist interference" and to go so far as to name the interventionists by pointing to the "CPSU leadership and some leadership groups within the CCP."

Even if Peking is continuing its efforts to bring the JCP under its control, at least the Party leadership has successfully asserted its right to independence from Moscow. A high-level Soviet delegation under CPSU Presidium member Mikhail Suslov visited Japan early in 1968 to bring about a normalization of inter-party relations. Talks were continued in Moscow in August of the same year. Official Japanese Communist communiques claim that the JCP has not given up its policy positions, that it has forced the CPSU to drop its support for Shiga's pro-Moscow splinter group and to officially acknowledge the Japanese Party's right to mutual "equality, independence, and non-intervention." These assertions seemed confirmed by an official Soviet communique published in *Pravda* August 15,1968, but subsequent events showed that the Soviets had not completely abandoned their support of the Shiga group. As a result, relations between the CPSU and the JCP once more deteriorated, reaching the breaking point in the summer of 1970.[6]

Impact on Party Policy

As indicated earlier, the Party's stance on issues contested by Moscow and Peking has evolved through a number of stages. Its latest decision was foreshadowed in a basic strategy document, the new program (or 1961 Thesis), which apparently was conceived in Peking. This orientation became clearer as specific issues posed by the Sino-Soviet conflict demanded that the various Communist parties take a public stand. The Japanese Communists proved unwilling to follow Khrushchev and condemn Albania. Neither did they go along with his handling of the Hungarian and Cuban crises, with Soviet-Yugoslav rapproachement, or with Soviet support for the Indian side in the border conflict with China.

Where the JCP stood on the Moscow-Peking spectrum in the midsixties was made clear when the nuclear question assumed paramount importance in Sino-Soviet relations and world affairs. The Japanese Communists refused to endorse the partial nuclear test ban treaty* which the Soviets had signed in 1963 over Chinese objections. Further, they gave hearty approval to the Chinese atomic test of 1964 and subsequent Chinese efforts to develop an independent nuclear potential. "Khrushchev" and "revisionism" became bad words in the Japanese Party's vocabulary as they had become in Peking.

None of this should be surprising. The Soviet strategy of peaceful coexistence, reflected in a willingness to reach certain understandings with the United States, could not have much appeal for the Japanese Communists. To them, U.S. power, intimately allied to the conservative forces in Japan, was the principal obstacle to Communist progress in Japan. There were also other considerations. Japanese Communists could not but be more sympathetic to Chinese policy positions, given the background of the Japanese Party leaders: their long underground

---

*This decision was taken at the Seventh Plenum of the JCP in October 1963. *Pravda* thereupon took the Japanese Communists to task. These events marked the beginning of the deterioration of relations between Moscow and Yoyogi.

existence and prison life, and their historic affinity for China and the Chinese Communists' much greater readiness to assist the Japanese Party, with Peking serving as home base and training ground for many JCP leaders and cadres. Racial considerations may also have entered into the Japanese Communist reaction to Sino-Soviet rivalry, particularly since the Chinese had stressed the Asian theme in their anti-Soviet propaganda and indoctrination.

In retrospect, however, the Japanese Communists, while agreeing with many Chinese Communist arguments against Khrushchev's policies, had persistent reservations about specific Chinese recommendations for Communist strategy in Japan. Even on international Communist policy there was no complete meeting of the minds. Disagreement, then and now, centered on two issues.

Both sides see U.S. "imperialism" as the principal enemy, but the Chinese Communists have been pressing other Asian parties as well as the Communist Party of Japan to accept the line of people's war and revolution by violence.[7] After the disastrous experience with violence in the 1950's, the Japanese Party is understandably leery of further experiments along this line. Its doubts have been reinforced by the failure of the Indonesian Communists, which many attribute to poor advice from Peking. Matters were not improved by Chinese attempts to compel the JCP to take the path of violence. The Chinese also seem to have overplayed their hand when they exhorted a group of young Japanese Party members visiting China on a "friendship exchange" of young people that they should heed the implications of Mao Tse-tung's dictum that political power grows out of the barrel of the gun. JCP leadership will no longer listen to such advice, considering it dangerous "leftist adventurism."

But suspicions of Chinese motivation in pressing the militant line go deeper. JCP leaders apparently wonder whether Peking's intent is not primarily to protect China's interests even at the risk of sacrificing its Japanese friends. The Chinese reiterate that a war with the United States is imminent and that before any attack against China comes, the U.S. position must be weakened by attacks against such U.S. strongholds as Japan. Nationalist sentiments have arisen in the Japanese Party as it has begun to think in terms of Japanese needs rather than foreign Communist demands. This clash of interests and nationalism has become increasingly apparent as the Japanese Communists have sought to re-examine their domestic strategy, aware that neither Soviet nor Chinese formulas fit Japan. Peking, in *Jen-min Jih-pao* (People's Daily),

February 16, 1968, took issue with the Japanese Party's new national security program, which insisted that Japan should have the right of self-defense. As *Akahata* (March 3, 1968) put it: "It is the right and duty of the Japanese people to fight when their sovereignty is violated, their land invaded, and their fundamental rights trampled down." This went contrary to the Socialist and Japanese pacifist views, and the Chinese Communists consider such a statement, even from the Communists, akin to the conservative Satō government's efforts to rearm Japan. As seen from Peking, the JCP's national defense program was "obviously . . . intended to bolster the Japanese reactionaries' expansionist policy of aggression," showing the "traitorous face of the Miyamoto clique." [8]

Just as serious—and broader in its implications—is a disagreement between the Chinese and the Japanese parties that has arisen over international Communist strategy. The Chinese have insisted that it is not possible or desirable to fight jointly with the "revisionist" Soviet Communists even though the latter aid the Vietnamese in their "national liberation struggle." Water and oil, they explain, do not mix. On the contrary, the Japanese Communists—like the North Koreans and of course the North Vietnamese—place the struggle against "U.S. imperialism" highest on the scale of priorities, higher even than the protection of "Marxist-Leninist purity" against "revisionist contamination."

The Japanese Communists have urged Moscow and Peking to set aside differences and unite in aiding the Vietnamese Communists.* They have insisted that the struggle in Vietnam is the crucial one and not, as the Chinese argue, any preparations for weakening the U.S. thrust against China. Whether this issue or Chinese interference in JCP affairs was the main reason for the complete breakdown of negotiations between the top Chinese Communist hierarchy and a high-level Japanese Communist mission to China led by Secretary General Miyamoto in the spring of 1966 is not certain.† There is no doubt, however, that this question was central in preventing the two parties from issuing even a joint communique and in accounting for the bitterness with which the

---

*Again, when Chairman Nosaka attended the funeral of Ho Chi Minh in Hanoi in September 1969, he tried to get the Soviets and the Chinese to set aside their differences for the sake of a joint effort in support of North Vietnam.

†The break between Yoyogi and Peking was made official by the Central Committee's Fourth Plenum of May 1966, although in this, as in other cases involving important JCP decisions, the rank and file were not told until months later in order to minimize factional problems within the Party.

Chinese press thereafter attacked the JCP. In a sense, the issue was whether ideological purity and the defense of China should have priority over a united effort of all Communist and "anti-imperialist forces" in support of the "liberation movement" in Vietnam.

The JCP's view of Party priorities was also reflected in the Japanese Communists' position on a Soviet-proposed international conference of Communists. As long as such a conference was likely to aggravate tensions within the Communist camp or become merely a forum for the excommunication of the Chinese Communists by Moscow, the JCP saw no good purpose in it. Neither Soviet pressure nor Suslov's persuasion has been able to budge the Japanese from this position. When the conference finally convened in Moscow, in June 1969, the Japanese Communists were absent. The Japanese Party's formula for a conference runs counter to both Soviet and Chinese recommendations: the JCP wants an international conference of "all anti-imperialist forces from the five continents." Its purpose would be to broaden the anti-imperialist front rather than to sharpen the confrontation between the two great Communist powers.

Pressures from Moscow have thus been unsuccessful in making the Japanese Communists abandon their basically anti-revisionist, moderate leftist stand on a whole range of policy issues on which Peking and Moscow disagree. On the other hand, Peking's leverage has also proved insufficient to rally the Japanese fully against the Soviet enemy.

Repercussions in the Ideological Realm

As Sino-Soviet tensions grew in the late 1950's and thereafter, the JCP sought for a while to prevent destructive ideological struggles within its own ranks by playing down the differences between the two camps and by including both Mao and Khrushchev in its pantheon. This position soon proved untenable, and the Party leadership was faced not merely with the practical and immediate consequences of the Sino-Soviet rift but with its philosophical and ideological implications.

As in other matters, the Party's reaction on the ideological plane to the broad issues raised by the Sino-Soviet controversy was closer to Peking's than Moscow's position. After a brief struggle, the pro-Moscow moderates and the structural-reform evolutionists lost out and were expelled from the Communist ranks. The Party remained dedicated to Marxist-Leninist orthodoxy and opposed to the "revisionist," pragmatic tendencies of the West European Communist parties. Despite Japan's advanced stage of modernization, the Japanese Communist response to the question of how to adapt Marxism to a twentieth century society was essentially negative.

During the early 1960's, therefore, Moscow's contribution to the Japanese Party's ideological baggage was limited to Lenin, and the JCP disseminated Mao's works in ever-increasing numbers. From the beginning of this Chinese ideological invasion, doubts were raised in Japan about the relevance of Mao's theories to Japanese conditions and thus implicitly about his claims to universality. As disagreements between the Japanese and Chinese parties developed, Mao's writings also disappeared from JCP reading lists. The Japanese Communists have since lashed out against the errors of Khrushchev and Mao, notably against "big-power chauvinism." Mao has fared somewhat better than Khrushchev in these attacks, but Mao's insistence on being acknowledged by even foreign parties as an infallible leader has rankled the Japanese Communists. They did not hesitate to denounce the cult of personality displayed by the Chinese Party at its Ninth Party Congress.

The shelves of loyal JCP members have now been cleared of all but the early Marxist classics and Lenin. The writings of Japanese such as the early Communist Katayama Sen and the present top JCP leadership have been added to the basic Japanese Communist library. Here, as in other areas of Japanese Communist activity, a certain degree of xenophobia and nationalism is making itself felt. There is now much talk about the "creative application of Marxism-Leninism to Japan." This may be merely the prelude to another attempt by Party intellectuals to reexamine Marxism-Leninism in the light of contemporary Japan. In the past, such attempts have invariably ended with a reassertion of orthodoxy and with the culprits' expulsion from the Party, but as younger leaders rise in the JCP, the Japanese Communists may go their own way, independent of Moscow and Peking in the realm of ideology as well.

The JCP in a World Context

The Japanese Communists' self-perceived position within the world Communist system has undergone a striking evolution in the past several years under the impact of the Sino-Soviet conflict on international communism. Well into the postwar period, the Japanese Communist Party was probably the least nationalist and assertive in its relations with the outside Communist world. It viewed itself as an integral part of a vast and developing Communist world system in which there was no place for nationalism or an independent path to Communist objectives. Moreover, it accepted a subordinate role vis-a-vis the motherland of communism, the Soviet Union, and agreed with Soviet leaders that a Communist victory in Japan as elsewhere could only come if all Communist forces recognized their duty to defend the Soviet system. More readily perhaps than other Communists, the Japanese Communists were willing to accept the thesis that what is good for the Soviet Union is also good for the Communist movements of other countries. During the prewar years in Japan the Party was weak and the state apparatus strong, so obviously the Communists could not hope to seize power without foreign support.

The Japanese began to change their view of their place in the Communist world system probably in the early postwar years, when Nosaka and his associates operated largely on their own, tasted freedom from foreign, i.e., Soviet controls, and were quite successful in building up a mass party without much foreign assistance. To judge by Nosaka's statements today, JCP leaders had gained sufficient confidence by then to visualize their position as one deserving autonomy within the world Communist movement.

The clash of Soviet and Chinese nationalisms and national interests— as reflected eventually in border clashes between the two countries— and the events in Hungary, in Tibet, and in Czechoslovakia must have provided further food for thought. Many Japanese Communist leaders were deeply troubled by these events, which clearly demonstrated that even Communist nations can have conflicting interests. Regarding events in Hungary and Czechoslovakia (which were considered quite different from the Tibetan case), the Japanese Communists felt that Soviet "great power chauvinism" was largely to blame for the display of Communist disunity.

On the other hand, the strategy of violence imposed on the JCP by Moscow and Peking in 1950 had caused the Japanese Communists not only to doubt the wisdom of their mentors but to suspect the purpose of that strategy. They wondered whether the JCP was not consciously being pushed into a strategy that might serve Soviet and Chinese but not Japanese interests. This suspicion must have grown as both Moscow and Peking began to interfere in JCP affairs more and more openly in their struggle for supremacy within the Communist world system. The Soviet intervention in Czechoslovakia (condemned by the JCP), the Soviet position on the Nuclear Non-Proliferation Treaty (opposed by the Japanese Party), Soviet insistence on its legitimate rights to the Kurile Islands, and the Sino-Soviet border incidents of 1969 all confirmed the Japanese Communists in their suspicions of the Soviet Union. But Mao's intervention in Japanese Party affairs convinced Japanese Communist leaders that both the Russians and the Chinese were "great power chauvinists" rather than Communist internationalists.

The Japanese Communists continue to place high value on the existence of a single Communist world system. But today the Japanese Party believes that such a system can no longer be composed of unequals, of leaders and followers, of teachers and disciples. The Party has grown up and is beginning to feel and behave like an independent entity. Analysis of Japanese Communist statements over the past decade shows a striking change in the vocabulary. Today, all major Party pronouncements dwell heavily on the need for independence and autonomy from foreign influence. They warn against "blindly following foreign examples," advocate the "creative application of Marxism-Leninism" to national conditions, and stress equality within the single Communist family of nations. As postwar Japan has demoted the head of the family from his all-powerful position, so has the JCP removed both its Communist mentors from their exalted status.

Of course, this evolution is not unique to the Communist Party of Japan (although it is perhaps more striking there because of the Party's long tradition of subordination to foreign Communist interests). During the past few years, the JCP has promoted relations with like-minded ruling parties in Asia—primarily North Korea and North Vietnam—and in Europe and elsewhere with parties that are seeking independence from Moscow and Peking while working for worldwide Communist unity in the struggle against "U.S. imperialism." Both North Korea and North Vietnam have asserted their national interests against pressures from Moscow and Peking to concentrate on the struggle against the "American enemy." In this they have found a strong ally in the Japanese Communists, who are now consulting with them on joint action and seeking to coordinate strategy. This is evident in the official pronouncements of the three Asian parties as well as in the comings and goings of their leaders.

For example, on the eve of Miyamoto's trip to Peking to thrash out the two parties' differences over domestic and international strategy, on December 7, 1965, *Akahata* published an article, "On the Strengthening of International Struggle Against Contemporary Revisionism and

American Imperialism," that was openly critical of the Chinese Communists. The previous day an article with identical arguments had been carried by the North Korean Communist Party organ. Before and after the crucial weeks of negotiations with Peking early in 1966, Miyamoto and his delegation traveled frequently to Hanoi and Pyongyang to consult with comrades there. Both the North Vietnamese and the North Korean parties issued joint communiques with the Japanese Communists demonstrating agreement with the Japanese view that the entire socialist camp should unite against the United States and implicitly urging China and the Soviet Union to lay aside their differences to join this struggle. Ties between the three parties have since been further strengthened.

This drawing together of Asian parties unwilling to join either of the two rival Communist powers had been accompanied by a broadening of Japanese Communist contacts with like-minded parties on other continents, particularly those of Italy, Rumania, and Cuba. In early 1968, by invitation, a Presidium-level JCP delegation visited Rumania and Korea to consult on whether to attend the Soviet-sponsored consultative meeting of Communist and Workers' parties in Budapest. It concluded that the purpose of unifying the Communist anti-American movement would not be served by JCP attendance. In 1969, the Japanese Communist Party further strengthened its ties with the independent-minded Rumanians and Italians through an exchange of high-level missions.

Important statements by the two Japanese Communist Party leaders suggest their current view of the world Communist system and their party's place in it. Addressing a meeting held to celebrate the forty-fifth anniversary of the Party, Nosaka said:

> Dear comrades! The autonomous and independent stand of our Party also has extremely important significance in the international arena. Both the international Communist movement and the Socialist camp today are faced with a great ordeal due to the erroneous currents of opportunism on both fronts—in short, modern revisionism and dogmatism and sectarianism. The chauvinist intervention in other parties and revolutionary movements by the CPSU leadership and a certain segment of the CCP have dealt a serious blow to the international Communist movement. . . . The difficulties which we face [as a result] . . . will turn out to be temporary and transitional and the movement will achieve militant unity at a new stage and on the basis of the autonomy and independence of all parties. [9]

A few days later, Miyamoto stressed once more that "although Japan's revolution is a link in the chain of the task of liberating the world's people, this liberation of the Japanese people must be carried out mainly by the Japanese people themselves." He then evoked the JCP's dreams of a new kind of Communist unity: "At present, the spontaneous unity of the independent Communist Parties which hold such views is a new form of proletarian internationalism and a new purpose of the international Communist movement." [10] In line with these views, the JCP condemned the 1968 Soviet intervention in Czechoslovakia and subsequently opposed all Soviet and Chinese attempts elsewhere to impose their rule on other Communist countries or parties.

*   *   *

In prewar times, the Japanese Communist Party was so weak and its standing within the international Communist movement so low that the Party's voice carried little weight in Moscow's Comintern councils. It was heard only when it conveniently confirmed Soviet views. This situation continued for a while after the war, both in Moscow and in Peking. Only the outbreak of the Sino-Soviet conflict has brought about a change, not only because altered conditions allowed the Japanese Party greater independence but because both the CPSU and the CCP began to vie for Japanese Communist support. Soviet failures (in Hungary, Cuba, and Czechoslovakia, for example) and Chinese difficulties (such as the problem of Tibet, the failure in Indonesia, the CCP's isolation within the Asian Communist context, and the strife and disruption caused by the Cultural Revolution) further encouraged the JCP to take a more active part in the formulation of international Communist policy.

These rather recent Japanese pressures on Moscow and Peking to conform to Japanese Communist wishes have been exerted primarily in two areas. In defending its autonomous status, the JCP has sought to discourage the Soviet and Chinese parties from strengthening their respective factions in Japan and from intervening in the Party's internal affairs. In this respect the JCP has been somewhat more successful with Moscow: the Soviet leaders have reduced their support for Shiga's pro-Moscow, anti-Party group, and have even tacitly accepted the JCP dictum that the dissidents' return to the Party is presently out of the question. Peking has not been convinced that the Japanese Party can and will defend its newly won independence. In 1968, relations between Yoyogi headquarters and Peking reached the breaking point. The JCP expelled Peking's friends (including secret members like "ambassador" Saionji), ordered a number of Party members to return from China, and eventually withdrew all its supporters from Peking. Meanwhile, the struggle against Chinese interference goes on.

Japanese Party leaders are also patiently trying to reestablish an international united front against the United States to help conclude the Vietnam war successfully. They seek to overcome Chinese resistance to such a front, which would have to include the Soviet Union, China's arch-enemy. As a means toward the united front and to soften Sino-Soviet differences, the JCP has been advocating an international anti-imperialist conference, at which each nation would be represented by "a unified delegation of all anti-imperialist democratic forces." Japanese Communists have been sent to consult with their Korean, Vietnamese, and Rumanian friends and also to urge comrades in France, Cuba, Poland, Italy, and other countries to participate in the conference and persuade Moscow and Peking to join. The prospects for the realization of this Japanese scheme seem doubtful because of Chinese resistance to any conference in which the Soviets are represented, but it is certainly a departure from tradition for the Japanese Communists to take the initiative in matters of international Communist policy.

*   *   *

In the preceding sections we have examined the Japanese Communist Party's reaction to the Sino-Soviet dispute and its effect on Party leadership, organization, and strategy. No doubt the conflict between Moscow and Peking has caused serious confusion within Japanese Party ranks and Japanese Communists have found it difficult to adjust to a world of Communist polycentrism. As we have shown above, however, a trend toward independent thinking has evolved out of the Party's inner turmoil. Thus, the Japanese Communists have sought to define their own party's position on important issues between Moscow and Peking. In the process, the JCP has come out on neither side, although it leans more toward Peking's philosophy.

The Japanese Communist leadership today generally rejects the

cluster of notions which the Chinese describe as "revisionism," including the Soviet emphasis on peaceful coexistence, on building the socialist system as a bulwark against "imperialism" rather than on seeking, as
the Chinese urge, to foster "national liberation movements." The Japanese Communists, like the Chinese, do not accept the Soviet view of the
socialist camp as a more important factor in history than "national
liberation movements." Certainly in their attitudes toward the United
States, the Chinese and the Japanese Parties have much in common.

It is on specifics rather than on principles, and on the ways in which
China attempts to carry out principles, that the Japanese disagree with
the Chinese. Thus, the Japanese object to Peking's indiscriminate pro-
motion of the dicta that "violent revolution is a universal law governing
the proletarian revolution" and "armed struggle is the highest form of
class struggle." Japanese Communist leaders argue that in Japan, at
least, these statements do not apply, although they do not rule out the
use of violence to gain power. It is rather that the Japanese Communists
have turned against the Chinese side in the Sino-Soviet conflict and
toward an independent position because the Chinese Communists have
so adamantly refused to make common cause with the Soviet Union in
the struggle against "U.S. imperialism," because at home and abroad
they have so ruthlessly and blindly advocated a single, inflexible strategic formula, and because they have claimed universality for Mao Tse-
tung's thought and practice. Chinese obduracy and militancy have
driven the Japanese Communists to call Mao an "anti-Marxist-Leninist."

Yet today, though the Japanese Communists are ideologically closer
to the Chinese Communists they enjoy better relations with the Soviets,
whose policies they disapprove of in a fundamental way. This paradoxi-
cal situation has not come about in a month or a year, but has resulted
from harsh treatment of the Japanese by Peking and a less intransigent
diplomacy by Moscow.

It should be noted that the present state of affairs may be a tempo-
rary one, that it may last only until the Chinese leaders accept the
notion that not all situations are amenable to Chinese solutions.
JCP-CCP relations could improve rather suddenly should the Chinese
leadership abandon the Red Guard pattern in its dealings with the
Japanese Communists. Such a possibility is suggested by the Japanese
Party's stress on the point that their quarrel is not with the Chinese
Communist Party, but only with an extremist "Mao Tse-tung clique."
That point was again made early in January 1970 by Chairman Nosaka,

who spoke of his party's friendly feelings toward the Chinese Communist Party and people.

*   *   *

Except for its contacts with the Indonesian party before that party was crushed by the military in 1965-66, the Japanese Communist Party's relations with other nonruling Communist parties have until recently been rather slight. This is attributable to several conditions: the geographic and political isolation of Japan, which until about a decade ago discouraged international contacts unless of high priority; the close relations between the JCP and the major ruling parties, particularly the CPSU, the CCP, and the Korean Workers' Party, which seemed to obviate the need for consultation with lesser parties; and the fact that other non-ruling Communist parties were either insignificant (like the Thai party), operated in very different circumstances (like the Indian party), or followed policies that were unacceptable to the JCP because of their "revisionist" taint (like most West European parties). Japanese Communist delegates thus appeared only occasionally at important national Communist congresses, and the impact of such visits appears to have been slight. With the JCP's increasing independence, Japanese representatives are now frequent guests in Western Europe and maintain closer liaison with other Asian and European non-ruling parties.

*   *   *

The Japanese Communists have always placed much emphasis on active participation in organizations that can be used as transmission belts for Communist propaganda at home and abroad. The JCP has therefore been well represented at international meetings of Communist sympathizers, not only of labor, professional, and cultural organizations, but all gatherings promoting the Communist theme of "defense of peace," such as anti-war and anti-nuclear rallies where, as the world's first victims of the atom bomb, Japanese delegates can speak with particular authority. With the increasingly autonomous orientation of the JCP, the Japanese Communists will no doubt play a more active and a more independent role in their relations with Communist-oriented organizations, especially since the Party's ambition in the international arena is to be the prime agent of a worldwide united front against "U.S. imperialism."

6: Principal Determinants of JCP Behavior

Like other political movements, the Japanese Communist Party bears the marks of an environment which has shaped its outlook and policies, its objectives and style of operations. The national environment underwent a drastic change about mid-point in the JCP's five decades of intermittent existence. Japan's defeat in World War II constitutes a sharp demarcation line both in Japan's history and in that of its Communist Party. Revived in 1945 after a long period of virtual extinction, the Japanese Communist Party was confronted with the need for adapting to an entirely new set of circumstances that were generally more favorable. This process is still under way, although today, more than two decades after the revival, we can draw certain conclusions about the direction in which the Communist movement in Japan is moving.

When founded in 1922, the JCP was a very junior offspring of the Japanese Socialist movement, which in turn was merely a minority group outside the mainstream of Japanese life. The members and leaders of this small Communist organization represented only a tiny fraction of Japanese society, and communism, for a number of reasons, remained a weak voice among the chorus of protesters in prewar Japan. This pronounced minority status of the Party, the feeling of weakness, and lack of mass support when confronted with the overwhelming power of the state affected the Party's style of operation, depriving it of flexibility, for there was always the danger that the tiny group might simply disintegrate in the face of hostile pressures. The Party thus carried over into the postwar period a tendency to be uncompromising, to consider itself a chosen instrument, and to protect its ideological purity in order not to be absorbed by that mainstream of socialist thought, the Japan Socialist Party.

The doctrinaire character of the JCP also owes much to its social composition. From its inception, intellectuals and quasi-intellectuals played the leading role in the Party and much of the time also made up the majority of its rank and file. The predominance of intellectuals

88

tended to divorce the Party from the realities of Japan and to orient it toward theoretical discussion and argument. The prewar Party was often beset by internal dissension stemming both from the frustrations of a hopeless-looking struggle for power and from the natural tendency of intellectuals to engage in ideological disputes. This absence of a mass base, specifically a peasant base, produced a Party that was isolated from Japanese reality and behaved accordingly. Only in the postwar period has the JCP begun to lose the character of a sectarian organization.

Probably the most influential aspect of the Japanese environment in shaping the outlook of the Party's leadership was the nature of the Japanese state apparatus. Virtually impregnable, it presented an insuperable obstacle to the growth of communism. Not only was the state equipped with an effective, repressive police system; it was also the agent of successful modernization and of the defense and expansion of Japanese power against Western countries, which had turned the rest of Asia into colonies. Thus the Japanese Communist Party faced a dilemma. Radical opposition to the imperial government's policies risked being equated with a lack of patriotism, which could be interpreted as an indication of foreign influence. At the same time, opposition to prewar Japan's emperor system meant certain persecution by the authorities and eventual imprisonment. If, on the other hand, the Communists recognized certain distinctive features and beliefs of prewar Japan's government, they were in danger of losing their identity; this eventually happened to the Socialists, who were absorbed into the maelstrom of Japanese ultra-nationalism. Not having anything to fight but indigenous imperialism rather than foreign, Western imperialism, the Japanese Communists were forced into opposing national policies that had long enjoyed massive popular support. Anti-colonialism and nationalism thus could not be mobilized for the Party's purposes as they were in China and the rest of Asia.

Apart from the legalization of the JCP, the greatest postwar environmental change affecting the Party is that it can now use nationalism in fighting the government, for U.S. influence in Japan is so strong and Japan's postwar dependence on the United States has been so great that it is possible to focus reviving Japanese nationalism on this issue. Nevertheless, even under the changed postwar circumstances, the Japanese Communist Party has found it difficult to pose as the spokesman for Japanese nationalism. The Socialists, with their strong indigenous roots, are better qualified for such a role than the Communists, about whom a foreign flavor still remains as a result of their prewar dependence on Soviet support.

Throughout its entire prewar life, the Japanese Communist Party was compelled to lead the furtive, conspiratorial existence of a secret organization. This experience, together with the long years most of the surviving Party leaders spent in prison or exile, has of course distorted the Party's outlook and profoundly affected its style of operations. On the other hand, those leaders who survived the war years in prison, having made a heavy investment in the cause of communism, are exceptionally tough and dedicated men.

But today only a small and rapidly decreasing fraction of the Party's membership shares any of these experiences. Recruited and for the most part even reared in postwar years, the Party's rank and file is the product of an open society where dissent is permitted and even protected by the state, where secret political and paramilitary operations seem incongruous, where nothing in the environment encourages a doctrinaire perspective or rigid adherence to a "universal truth"—Marxism-Leninism or whatever—and where discipline of the kind the prewar Party demanded and the leadership still requires is difficult to obtain and even more difficult to maintain.

The liberalized postwar environment has created something of a generation gap in the Party. It has also put pressure on the Party leadership to soften the JCP's characteristic features inherited from prewar years and to integrate the Party into the Japanese environment. External developments also have encouraged this "naturalization" of the JCP.

CROSS-NATIONAL DETERMINANTS

Two major external factors had a powerful impact on the prewar Japanese Communist movement: Marxism-Leninism as interpreted in Moscow, which provided the Party with its ideological base; and direct Soviet influence, which determined the JCP's leadership and organization as well as its strategy and policies. Marxism-Leninism took a particularly strong hold in Japan, where the intellectual is more than elsewhere inclined to seek "perfect" and "universal" explanations and solutions, where foreign theories and doctrines have been accepted rather uncritically as part of modern Japan's process of borrowing from the West, and where social and economic conditions during the prewar industrialization period resembled those predicted by Marx when he spoke of an exploitative capitalist system. Marxism-Leninism in its most dogmatic form thus became the Japanese Party's philosophy. Throughout the prewar period it was treated by the Japanese Communists as a sacred revelation. Blind faith in the omniscience of Moscow, on the other hand, allowed the Japanese Communists to accept the zigzags of Soviet interpretations of Marxism, for only those remained in the Party who were able to accept Moscow as the source of all wisdom.

This strong Soviet influence over the Japanese Party began nearly fifty years ago, when the Soviet-controlled Comintern brought the Japanese Party to life, and it continued throughout the prewar years until conditions made contacts between Japan and the Soviet Union impossible. The Japanese Communist Party therefore carried over into the postwar era a tradition of loyalty to Moscow and unquestioned acceptance of foreign guidance. The great majority of prewar Communist leaders in Japan were either Moscow-trained or had intimate connections with the Soviet Union. These same men were also responsible for reviving the Communist Party after the war.

Yet the postwar period brought important changes in the domestic conditions of Japan and in its international environment. These changes have profoundly affected the two external determinants of Japanese Communist behavior. The faith of Japanese intellectuals (including the Communist intellectuals) in Marxism-Leninism has been put to a severe test as social and political change in such advanced countries as those of Western Europe, the United States, and Japan has contradicted Marx's and Lenin's predictions. The liberal climate of postwar Japan has encouraged the challenging of all accepted truths and theories—including the foundations of Marxist-Leninist revolutionary thought.

The validity of Marxism and its Soviet form has been increasingly and openly questioned by a large segment of Japan's educated class, and the effect is beginning to be felt even within the Marxist-Leninist Japanese Communist Party, as is evidenced by inner-Party discussions and by a number of defections among Party sympathizers. Marxism continues to be the most widely accepted theory of social change in Japan, but it is no longer an unquestioned guide for the intellectual rebel, and the Japanese Communists cannot help but be affected by this.

Ideological developments abroad have, of course, contributed to the questioning of the validity of Marxism and to attempts in Japan to "adapt" Marx to modern conditions. Structural reform theories and many of the revisions that have been discussed or accepted by Marxist intellectuals abroad have had their impact in Japan: the Party split occurred at least in part over the structural reform theories of Togliatti and other European Communists. The more recent tendency in the Japanese Communist Party to refuse to follow blindly Moscow's or Peking's formulas and the resulting efforts to "creatively apply Marxism-Leninism to Japanese conditions" undoubtedly will undermine the position of the dogmatists in the Japanese Party and reduce the hold of orthodoxy. This may be a slow process, but the symptoms can already be discerned.

The outbreak and intensification of the Sino-Soviet conflict has also encouraged conditions in which the Japanese Party's traditional reliance on Moscow for guidance had to give way to critical evaluation. The same applies to the Japanese Communists' relations with Peking. In 1950, Japanese Communist leaders still unquestioningly accepted the orders emanating from Moscow and Peking to adopt a new strategy more suited to the defense of Soviet and Chinese interests. Today, only two decades later, the Japanese Communist leaders—largely the same men who have led the Party since prewar days—steadfastly defend their positions against criticism by both Moscow and Peking. As a new generation moves into Party leadership, we may assume that this trend will intensify.

Japanese Communists now realize that the conditions under which the Soviet and Chinese Communists succeeded in seizing power are not relevant as models for Japan. The very fact that Moscow and Peking disagree over "correct" Communist strategy weakens confidence in their wisdom and policy prescriptions. The several failures suffered by both the Soviet and the Chinese Communists in their dealings with communism outside their countries raises further doubts in Japanese leaders' minds. Finally, a developing nationalist sentiment stimulated by the spread of Communist movements everywhere and encouraged by the changing mood of Japan discourages the JCP from following its tradition of absolute obedience to foreign guidance.

As with other Communist Parties, however, this poses a severe dilemma for the Japanese Communists. That they are firm believers in the desirability and even necessity of building a Communist world system is evidenced in every major Japanese Communist policy statement of recent years. But how is such a system to be built, and how is the universality of Marxist-Leninist thought to be preserved if each Party develops its own interpretation of the allegedly universal truth of Marxism-Leninism through efforts to apply that theory "creatively"? Where and by whom is the line to be drawn beyond which the universality of the system becomes endangered and adaptation can no longer be permitted?

7: Summary and Conclusions

The Japanese Communist Party was established fifty years ago, with Comintern assistance, by a small group of radical Socialists who expected to launch a mass movement that would overthrow the existing order and build on its ruins a new society along Marxist-Leninist lines. For the most part intellectuals—theorists and idealists rather than activists or politicians—the leaders of the Japanese Communist movement had given little thought to how, exactly, they would realize their objectives in the face of a powerfully entrenched and extremely efficient state apparatus. They seem to have relied to a large extent on the alleged inevitability of communism's victory thoughout the world and on the aid and advice they were to receive from the Communist power center, Moscow.

In the prewar years, condemned to an illegal, conspiratorial existence, the small Communist Party—counting never more than 1,000 members and most of the time much less—made no visible headway toward its original goals. Yet a hard core of Japanese Communists—by war's end mostly in prison or in exile—never abandoned faith in Marxism-Leninism or the conviction that the Japanese people would eventually turn to them to build a Communist Japan.

Under radically different and considerably more favorable conditions, the JCP reemerged into the Japanese political arena after the war as a legitimate political party. Compared to its prewar record, the JCP has been quite successful in the two decades of its postwar existence. Today it counts some 300,000 members and ten times that number of sympathizers. It can expect to poll upwards of three million votes representing 5 percent or more of the electorate. The Party operates cells and branches throughout the country, has a foothold among labor and in various leftist organizations, holds a rather strong position among certain groups of government workers, and has some backing among small business.

Yet, despite all these accomplishments, the JCP remains a comparatively minor factor in the Japanese political picture. It is not the only or even the major source of political and social protest. It has little leverage in the Diet, nor is it strong enough to otherwise affect Japanese policy directly. To be effective, it must operate as a component of a larger

94

popular front with the much stronger Socialists or a combination of opposition elements. So far it has failed to build such a front except in a few instances, and then only on a temporary basis.

As a result, the JCP has scaled back its original ambitions in accordance with a more sober appraisal of Japanese reality. Instead of aiming at direct access to power and total victory, the Party appears now satisfied with the more modest intermediate goal of forging a coalition of all "progressive and democratic forces" in which it would play an important if not predominant role. An objective appraisal of Japanese conditions does not hold out much hope for the Japanese Communist Party to exercise in the foreseeable future significant political power in Japan. Its strength and appeal reside in areas none of which seems as promising today as in the past, nor does the future look more encouraging.

The ideology of Marxism-Leninism and the Party's principle of allowing for only one path, one "correct solution" in all situations, together with its strong faith in the inevitability and universality of Marxist-Leninist principles, has provided its adherents with a feeling of security in a world of rapid change. But the relevance of this ideology (which the Party at any rate does not monopolize in Japan, for there is another Marxist party) is being increasingly questioned today. Its universality is in doubt, and so is the dogma of inevitability. Moreover, another charismatic political movement, the Kōmeitō, provides a competing outlet for the contemporary Japanese search for inner security. Increasingly, pragmatism is replacing dogmatism among Japanese intellectuals, who constitute the politically most effective and vocal group on which Japanese communism can draw for support.

The appeal of communism is said to lie also in the promise it holds out to those who suffer from the social and economic tensions generated by modernization. But social and economic problems of the majority of the Japanese people are being solved successfully, and the very real difficulties the lower-income groups experienced before the war are disappearing as Japan rapidly advances toward unprecedented prosperity and social mobility. In this age of mass communications, most Japanese are fully aware that their social and economic environment provides more ease, justice, and freedom than is available to the citizen in the Soviet Union or Communist China.

Finally—and in contrast to the prewar situation—the Communists appear to enjoy opportunities for capitalizing on nationalist sentiments.

The Japanese government is vulnerable to attacks directed against the predominant U.S. military and economic position in Japan at a time when the Japanese people are developing a strong desire to go their own independent way without owing their security to the protection of a foreign power. But here, too, the concerns at issue between Japan and the United States—such as the future of Okinawa and of U.S. bases in Japan—are being resolved through mutual accommodation. It seems unlikely that in the next decade the U.S. position in Japan will provide as vulnerable a target for Communist nationalist propaganda as it has in the recent past.

An analysis of the potential support groups for the Japanese Communists does not suggest major shifts in the present balance for the near future. Young intellectuals are less and less drawn to Marxist theories. The same appears to be true of organized labor, which is rapidly improving its economic condition, shedding its highly politicized behavior, and beginning to act as an economic interest group aiming at economic rather than political gain. Nor does the JCP have much prospect of improving its standing with the Japanese farmer, who generally owns his land and benefits increasingly from Japanese prosperity—insofar as he has not already joined the migration to the cities.

There is, of course, the possibility that the Party, frustrated in its efforts to make headway by legal means, might return to violent methods. But the Japanese state has survived military defeat in astonishingly good condition. With the vast majority of the Japanese people supporting democratic procedures and with the degree of alienation from the existing system rather low among all but a few, the government could certainly count on popular support if it had to crush a Communist coup attempt. Moreover, it is difficult to see what effective instruments the Japanese Communists could use for a coup: the police and military forces of the government are strong and loyal; the labor unions are largely under Socialist or Democratic Socialist control; and the majority of the Party members themselves—who constitute a small minority at any rate—are neither trained for nor inclined toward armed struggle along Chinese lines.

It could be argued, however, that the growing trend among the Japanese Communists to make of their movement a force that is truly independent of foreign influence and dedicated to the defense of the Japanese national interest will allow the Party to develop a real mass following, well beyond anything it has been able to attract in the past.

Such a trend toward "naturalization" already is apparent and is beginning to pay off at the polls. But it seems quite unlikely that such a policy could produce dramatic changes in the political balance within the next few years.

Looking to the future of Japapanese communism, a major factor will be the fate of the rival Japan Socialist Party, which until recently seemed the natural source of opposition to the conservative postwar government. But today its fate is uncertain as unrealistic policy positions, inept political behavior, and weak organization begin to take their toll. If the JSP succumbs to its traditional internal divisions, the Communists may be the principal beneficiaries. But the strong anti-Communist sentiments of many Socialists would seem to set limits on a shift of support to the Communists; at any rate, the absorption of traditional Socialist strength by the Communists would necessitate a long process of continued naturalization of the JCP. Clearly the Communists would have to choose the parliamentary path to power and abandon their present ambivalent attitude on this point. Should 'the JCP develop into a genuinely evolution-minded Japanese party, its attraction could increase substantially, especially if meanwhile the rival Kōmeitō were to decline. How far the Japanese Communists would be able to advance toward power even then would depend on the degree to which the conservative government could continue to solve successfully Japan's social and economic problems and the domestic or international difficulties it must face.

Insurmountable difficulties appear unlikely today, but cannot, of course, be ruled out entirely. A world economic crisis, with grave consequences to Japan, is not inconceivable. There is also the possibility that the intermittent erosion of conservative strength at the polls could reach the point where a coalition government would become inevitable. In an emerging center/left or leftist coalition, a moderate Communist Party with an improved popular image might be allowed to participate. Even then, it seems rather unlikely that such sharing of governmental power would offer the Japanese Communists an opportunity to grasp the levers of command. No doubt in a coalition the Party, even if it should continue to gain in strength, would still be relegated to a junior position, and the command of power would remain out of its reach.

Chronology

1921	Apr.- Sept.	Comintern representatives visit Japan to select promising young men for participation in Far Eastern People's Congress and to prepare for establishment of a Japanese Communist Party.
1922	Jan.- Feb.	Far Eastern People's Congress held in Moscow with participation of Japanese, including Katayama Sen and Tokuda Kyūichi. Japanese delegates leave with funds and instructions from Comintern.
	Jul. 15	First Japanese Communist Party formed secretly in Tokyo and recognized at the end of the year by Fourth Congress of Comintern.
1923	June	First "Communist Incident" involving arrest of most Japanese Communists.
1924	Spring	Dissolution of Communist Party. Disapproved by Comintern.
1925		Enactment of Peace Preservation Law directed mainly against Communist activities. First applied toward end of year. Fukumoto Kazuo emerges as leading Communist theoretician.
1926	Mar.	Labor-Farmer Party established.
	Dec.	JCP re-established after return of Tokuda from Moscow.
1927		Factional struggle within JCP. Comintern establishes special committee to deal with "Japanese question," adopts program for Japan (1927 Thesis) and appoints new JCP Central Committee, removing Fukumoto for his criticism. Communist infiltration of Labor-Farmer Party.

1927	Feb.	Japanese Communists begin to issue the illegal Party organ *Akahata* (Red Flag). The Communist Tokuda Kyūichi runs in the national elections as candidate of the Labor-Farmer Party.
1928	Mar.	Mass arrest of Communists and Communist sympathizers, followed by return of Japanese Communist trainees from Soviet Union.
	Apr.	Labor-Farmer Party dissolved by the Government.
	June	Peace Preservation law amended to include death penalty.
	Oct.	New thesis drafted under Comintern guidance. JCP is to become mass party.
1929	Apr.	Another wave of Communist mass arrests.
1930	Jan.-July	JCP adopts policy of armed violence. Organization crushed by police action.
	Nov.	Comintern sends replacements from among Japanese students in Moscow to Japan to reorganize Party.
1931		New Central Committee formed. Nosaka Sanzō (Party Chairman in 1970) sent to Comintern. Committee issues new policy guide, 1931 Draft Thesis. Party revitalized. Communist activity in host of front organizations.
1932	Mar.-May	Comintern criticizes 1931 Thesis. Replaced by 1932 Thesis urging bourgeois-democratic revolution. *162438*
	Oct.	Mass arrests of Communists followed by return of new Comintern trainees to implement 1932 Thesis.
1933		Continued arrests of Communists replaced by such new leaders as Miyamoto Kenji (Presidium Chairman in 1970) and

1933 (Cont.)   Hakamada Satomi (key figure in JCP in
                                      1970). First important defections from
                                      Communist leaders' ranks. Symptoms of
                                      Party's disintegration.

1934-35   Despite Nosaka's efforts to strengthen
                                      Party from abroad (Moscow and New
                                      York), organization disintegrates due to
                                      police repression, lack of leaders, internal
                                      dissension.

1936   Nosaka in letter to Party calls for popular
                                      front in line with Comintern policy. Mass
                                      arrest of Communists later that year ends
                                      organized, nationwide Communist activ-
                                      ity in Japan until JCP's revival in 1945.

1937-41   Small Communist groups emerge, but are
                                      soon crushed by police. Nosaka moves to
                                      Yenan (April 1940) to work with Mao
                                      Tse-tung. Opens Japanese Peasants' and
                                      Workers' School with prisoners of war.

1943   Comintern dissolved.

1944-45   Nosaka establishes Japanese People's
                                      Liberation League. Addresses Seventh
                                      Congress of Chinese Communist Party.

The Postwar Communist Movement

1945   Oct.   At direction of Allied authorities, Com-
                                      munist leaders (including Tokuda, Shiga,
                                      Miyamoto) released from prison. Commu-
                                      nist Party allowed to reconstitute itself as
                                      a legal political organization. First issue
                                      of postwar *Akahata* appears.

                Dec.   Fourth Congress of JCP adopts action
                                      program, Party rules, elects Central Com-
                                      mittee, Tokuda as Secretary-General.

1946   Jan.   Nosaka returns from China.

                Feb.   Fifth JCP Congress

                Apr.   JCP participates for first time legally in
                                      elections. Polls 3.8 percent of total vote.

1947	Feb.	General strike called off on order of Supreme Commander Allied Powers.
	Dec.	Sixth JCP Congress.
1949	Jan.	JCP polls three million votes and close to 10 percent of total vote in national elections.
1950	Jan.	Cominform journal criticizes JCP's moderate policy of "peaceful revolution." Party turns toward strategy of violence and radicalism.
	June	Central Committee members purged by Supreme Commander, *Akahata* suspended, Party leaders move underground and abroad (mostly China).
	Oct.	Adoption by JCP of 1951 Thesis.
1950 to mid-1950's		JCP under Peking influence and direction.
1952	Apr.	Peace treaty goes into effect. Japan independent.
	May 1	*Akahata* reappears. Large-scale riots in Tokyo.
	July	Anti-Subversive Activities Law adopted.
1955		JCP abandons strategy of violence. Tokuda's death in China announced.
1958	July-Aug.	Seventh JCP Congress. Nosaka elected Party Chairman, Miyamoto Secretary-General.
1959		Joint JCP statement with Korean and Chinese parties.
1960		Active Communist role in anti-security pact movement. Largest postwar political mass movement. Hakamada heads JCP delegation to Moscow Conference of Communist Parties.

1961	July	Eighth JCP Congress adopts new program.
	Oct.	Nosaka represents JCP at Twenty-second Congress of CPSU. Withholds endorsement of Khrushchev policies. Subsequently JCP swings increasingly toward support of Peking in the Sino-Soviet conflict.
1963	Oct.	Seventh Plenum of JCP refuses to endorse partial nuclear test ban treaty. Strong JCP identification with Peking policies.
1964	Feb.-Mar.	JCP representative Hakamada confers in Moscow, Peking, and Hanoi, followed by exchanges of letters between CPSU and JCP spelling out disagreements.
	May	Shiga expelled from JCP because of endorsement of partial nuclear test ban treaty.
	Nov.	Ninth JCP Congress.
1965		JCP moves toward position of autonomy from both Moscow and Peking.
1966	Feb.-Mar.	JCP delegation headed by Miyamoto visits North Vietnam, China and North Korea.
	May	Break between JCP and Peking is made official at Fourth Central Committee Plenum.
	June	JCP delegation issues joint communique with Rumanian CP.
	Sept.	Purge of pro-Peking Party members begins, accompanied by bitter exchanges between Yoyogi and Peking.
	Oct.	Tenth JCP Congress. Emphasis on Party's autonomy.
1967	Jan.	JCP polls 2.2 million votes.

| 1968 | Jan. | JCP proclaims its stand on Japan's national security policy. |

Feb. Joint communique regarding talks between CPSU and JCP. In subsequent meetings between the two parties, the JCP upholds its claim to autonomy from foreign influence. At the same time, JCP expels radical pro-Peking Party members.

1969 Dec. JCP polls 3.2 million votes in national elections.

1970 July Eleventh JCP Congress. Party Presidium and Central Committee expanded. Miyamoto Kenji elected to newly created key policy post of Presidium Chairman. Nosaka Sanzō remains Central Committee Chairman. Forty-year-old Fuwa Tetsuzō elected to seven-member Permanent Presidium and appointed Chief of the Party Secretariat. New Party regulations adopted. JCP affirms its autonomous stand.

Notes

EDITOR'S INTRODUCTION

1. V. O. Key, Jr., *Politics, Parties, and Pressure Groups*, 2nd ed. (New York: Crowell, 1953), p. 223.

2. *The Appeals of Communism* (Princeton: Princeton University Press, 1954).

3. *The Politics of Despair* (New York: Collier, 1962).

4. *Guerrilla Communism in Malaya* (Princeton: Princeton University Press, 1956).

5. Pye, op. cit., p. 344; Hugh Seton-Watson, *From Lenin to Khrushchev* (New York: Praeger, 1961), p. 320.

6. Seton-Watson, *ibid.*, p. 294.

7. Maurice Duverger, *Political Parties* (London: Methuen, 1954).

8. *The Theory of Social and Economic Organization* (Glencoe: Free Press, 1947).

9. *Modern Political Parties* (Chicago: University of Chicago Press, 1956).

10. *African Political Parties* (Baltimore: Pelican, 1960).

11. "Single Party Systems in West Africa," *American Political Science Review*, LV (1961), pp. 294-307.

12. "Authoritarian and Single Party Tendencies in African Politics," *World Politics*, XV, No. 2 (January 1963).

13. *Political Change in Underdeveloped Countries* (New York: Wiley, 1962); see also Colin Leys, "Models, Theories, and the Theory of Political Parties," *Political Studies*, VII (1959), pp. 127-46; Neil A. McDonald, *The Study of Political Parties* (New York: Doubleday, 1956); and Charles E. Merriam and Harold F. Grosnell, *The American Party System*, 4th ed. (New York: Macmilliam, 1949).

CHAPTER I: THE PREWAR PAST

1. For a detailed account of the role of the Comintern in the founding of the JCP, see Rodger A. Swearingen and Paul F. Langer, *Red Flag in Japan: International Communism in Action, 1919-1951* (Cambridge, Mass.: Harvard University Press, 1952).

2. For an excellent and detailed treatment of the prewar history of the Japanese Communists, see George M. Beckmann and Genji Okubo, *The Japanese Communist Party, 1922-1945* (Stanford, Cal.: Stanford University Press, 1969).

CHAPTER II: POSTWAR ROLE AND ORGANIZATION

1. This conclusion is not universally accepted. The well-informed Japanese political journalist Murata Kiyoaki, known for his work on extremist movements, places the figure of clandestine membership at a substantial percentage of the total membership. He believes that 2,000-3,000 intellectuals serve the Party effectively in this capacity and that quite a few have infiltrated the various agencies of the Japanese government where politically and technically sensitive work is being done. (As an instance of clandestine Party membership Murata mentions the case of Saionji Kinkazu, who served as something of an ambassador of the Japanese peace movement in Peking and was the liaison between all leftist Japanese visitors and the Chinese Communist Party hierarchy until the JCP cut its ties with him in 1967 over the issue of the JCP's criticism of Maoist policies.) See *Japan Times*, March 12, 1967.

2. See, for example, *Akahata*, October 26, 1966.

3. For profiles of leading Party officials in the early 1950's (who for the most part remain prominent today), see Swearingen and Langer, *Red Flag in Japan*. . . .

4. As quoted from Japanese government sources by Hans H. Baerwald in "The Japanese Communist Party—Yoyogi and Its Rivals," in Robert A. Scalapino (ed.), *The Communist Revolution in Asia* (Englewood Cliffs, N.J.: Prentice-Hall, 1965).

CHAPTER IV: JCP CONFLICT AND INTEGRATION WITH ITS NATIONAL ENVIRONMENT

1. Figures and assessments provided hereafter must be considered approximate, since the composition of such organizations, by nature fluctuates constantly. The following data represent a composite of

authoritative reports, largely from Japanese government sources but drawing also on Party publications and on studies by Japanese specialists. To facilitate an overview of the situation, organizations in which the Japanese Communists play an important role are arranged in three categories: occupational, special groups, and organizations devoted to specific issues.

2. For a good discussion of the radical Japanese student movement, see Sunada Ichirō, "The Thought and Behavior of Zengakuren: Trends in the Japanese Student Movement," *Asian Survey*, June 1969.

CHAPTER V: JCP CONFLICT AND INTEGRATION WITH THE INTERNATIONAL ENVIRONMENT

1. In its letter of April 18, 1964, to the JCP Central Committee, the Central Committee of the CPSU placed the blame for this open Soviet intervention in JCP affairs on Stalin personally ("...undertaken on the personal initiative of Stalin..."). See *Partiinaya Zhizn*, No. 14, 1964.

2. Nosaka Sanzō, "My Answer," *Chūō Kōron*, November 1955.

3. The previously quoted 1964 letter of the CPSU to the JCP Central Committee reflects Moscow's surprise: "For the first time in the history of relations between our Parties, representatives of the Central Committee of the JCP declared that they have no unity with the CPSU." Two years later, it was Peking's turn to be surprised.

4. On January 2, 1970, *Peking Review* reported that the pro-Peking "National Council of the Japanese Communist Party (Left)" had transformed itself into the "Communist Party of Japan (Left)." Despite the change of name, the pro-Peking Communists remain numerically weak even if they can count on Chinese financial and other support. This is even more true of the pro-Moscow Communist group under Shiga Yoshio.

5. *Akahata*, July 16, 1967.

6. In 1971, Moscow had second thoughts and once more took a conciliatory stand. In March 1971, both sides reaffirmed the 1968 understanding. As a result, the JCP sent an official delegation to the 24th Congress of the CPSU.

7. Secretary General Miyamoto told *Akahata* (July 28, 1967) that the Chinese had expressed the view that "the military strength of imperialism can be diverted more effectively by tens of thousands of

people armed with weapons than by one million party members of mass movements."

8. *Jen-min Jih-pao*, February 16, 1968.

9. *Akahata*, July 16, 1967.

10. See *Akahata*, July 28, 1967.

Bibliography

WESTERN LANGUAGE MATERIALS

With the exception of a number of articles in *Pravda* and other Soviet publications, which can provide some idea of Soviet interpretations of Japanese Communist Party affairs, virtually the entire useful Western literature on the subject is in the English language. Currently, no systematic documentary collection on the JCP exists in a Western language apart from the irregularly issued translations from the Japanese Communist Press contained in the relevant series (especially International Communist Developments and Translations on East Asia and on Southeast Asia) of the Joint Publications Research Service of the U.S. Government, available in most larger university collections. These translations go back only about one decade, however. (Two collections of translated materials on the history and policies of the JCP have been in preparation for some time by specialists at the University of Southern California.)

Books, Essays, and Articles

Baerwald, Hans H. "The Japanese Communist Party—Yoyogi and Its Rivals," in Robert A. Scalapino (ed.), *The Communist Revolution in Asia*. Englewood Cliffs, N.J.: Prentice-Hall, 1965; second edition, 1969. A brief but comprehensive survey.

Beckmann, George M. and Genji Okubo. *The Japanese Communist Party, 1922-1945*. Stanford, Cal.: Stanford University Press, 1969. The most complete treatment of the prewar Party. Includes key documents in translation, biographical sketches of Communist leaders, a chronology, and an extensive bibliography.

"Concerning the Situation in Japan," *For a Lasting Peace, For a People's Democracy*, January 6, 1950. The Comintern's vitriolic attack against Nosaka's strategy.

"Immediate Demands of Communist Party of Japan—New Programme," *For a Lasting Peace, For a People's Democracy*, November 23, 1951.

Hirotsu, Kyōsuke. "Isolation of Communist China and Japan Communist Party," *Review*, March 1967.

108

Langer, Paul F. "Communism in Independent Japan," in Hugh Borton (ed.), *Japan Between East and West*. New York: Harper, 1957. Discusses postwar JCP strategy, leadership, and organization as well as policies in the domestic and international context of the 1950's.

Langer, Paul F. "Independence or Subordination: The Japanese Communist Party Between Moscow and Peking," in Doak Barnett (ed.), *Communist Strategies in Asia*. New York and London: Praeger, 1963. An analysis of the JCP's international behavior written at a time when the JCP seemed to be wavering between its traditional dependence on foreign guidance and a more independent position. Useful notes.

Scalapino, Robert A. *The Japanese Communist Movement, 1920-1966*. Berkeley and Los Angeles: University of California Press, 1967. The most recent and comprehensive study of the subject. Draws on Japanese and Western sources.

Swearingen, Rodger A. and Paul F. Langer. *Red Flag in Japan: International Communism in Action, 1919-1951*. Cambridge, Mass.: Harvard University Press, 1952. A pioneer study based on a large body of original Japanese source materials.

Tsukahira, Toshio G. *The Postwar Evolution of Communist Strategy in Japan*. Cambridge, Mass.: Center for International Studies, M.I.T., 1954. Still valuable for its penetrating analysis.

During the 1960's, the Japanese Communist Party published a *Bulletin-Information for Abroad* with useful translated source materials. This publication, discontinued for a while, is currently (1970) again being issued. At least one Japanese research organization, the KDK Institute, issues a bulletin entitled *KDK Information* (monthly) in English, which provides regular coverage of the JCP. Relevant articles are occasionally found in Western language periodicals, especially the following: *Asian Survey, China Quarterly, Est et Ouest, Peking Review, Pacific Affairs,* and *Problems of Communism.*

JAPANESE LANGUAGE SOURCES

Since gaining legal status after the Second World War, the Japanese Communist Party (JCP) has issued a vast number of publications regarding its prewar and postwar history, strategy, and policies, as well as numerous collections of foreign Communist Party materials for the information and education of its own members and sympathizers. Despite this voluminous literature, we still lack satisfactory data on such important matters as the background of JCP leadership, organizational issues, the decision-making process, and factional problems. These gaps can be partly filled by consulting the vast body of documentary and interpretive materials issued by the security and other agencies of the Japanese government. Accounts by dissident JCP members and by knowledgeable sympathizers and observers of Japanese Communist Party life provide additional information.

The following is a selective listing of sources emanating from the JCP and its auxiliary organizations. It is limited to postwar materials which can be found in the major U.S. collections of Asian revolutionary literature, such as those of the Hoover Institution at Stanford University and the Library of Congress.

Major JCP periodicals (circulation figures as claimed by the Party or given by other authoritative Japanese sources).

Akahata (Red Flag), Official Party daily. Currently also available in monthly reduced print edition. Circulation, in late 1969, ca. 400,000. Circulation of special Sunday edition, 1.4 million.

Zen'ei (Vanguard). Official JCP monthly emphasizing problems of Communist theory and strategy. Circulation in late 1969, ca. 90,000.

Bunka Hyōron (Cultural Review). Monthly. Contents as described by title. Circulation in late 1969, 15,000.

Gikai to Jichitai (Parliament and Self-Government). Monthly. Contents as described by title. Circulation in 1969, probably 15,000.

Sekai Seiji Shiryō (Materials on World Politics). Monthly. Contains important policy documents and statements issued by other Communist parties, both ruling and non-ruling. Selected for JCP members' study and reference. Circulation in late 1969, probably 35,000.

Gekkan Gakushū (Monthly Study). For education, training, and self-improvement of Party members. Circulation in 1969, probably 110,000.

Gakusei Shimbun (Student Newspaper). Weekly. Circulation in 1969, estimated at 20,000.

Minshu Seinen Shimbun (Democratic Youth Newspaper). Weekly. Circulation in late 1969, ca. 300,000.

Collections of documents

The full text of important Party documents is published in the official daily *Akahata* and, to a lesser extent, in the Party monthly *Zen'ei*, which puts out special issues containing collections of Party documents on such occasions as Party congresses or in connection with particular policy problems and themes. In addition, the Party issues in book form, at irregular intervals, collections of selected Party documents (usually entitled "Resolutions and Decisions"), arranged in chronological order. The most extensive of these collections is *Nihon Kyōsantō Ketsugi Kettei-shū* (JCP Resolutions and Decisions), which by the spring of 1970 had reached 20 volumes. A similar serial publication, *Nihon Kyōsantō Jūyō Rombun-shū* (Collection of Important JCP Documents), in late 1969 was in its seventh volume. Further, Party documents are reprinted in the semi-official (government-sponsored) monthly *Kōan Jōhō*) (Information on Public Order). Reprints of JCP documentary materials are also periodically issued by publishers (such as Nikkan Rōdō Tsūshinsha) which reportedly are close to the security agencies of the Japanese government. (For the most complete collection of prewar Communist documentation, see the massive volumes 14 and 15 of *Gendai-shi Shiryō* (Materials on Contemporary History) published by Misuzu Shobo, Tokyo, in 1964-65.

Books

There exists a vast body of Japanese interpretive literature on the subject of the JCP authored by Party leaders and sympathizers, as well as by dissident former Party members and writers whose ideological positions range from sympathetic to frankly anti-Communist, among them several useful books authored by former members of Japanese security agencies. None of this extensive literature is available in English translation.

Index

DATE DUE

GAYLORD			PRINTED IN U.S.A